Kindred Spirits

stories, passions & portraits from
the heart of community

Island Time Press
P.O. Box 1633
Anacortes, WA 98221

ISBN 0-9700025-0-5

Library of Congress Catalog Card Number: 00-105605

Design and Layout:
Lanphear Design, Snohomish, Washington

Printed in China
by Oceanic Graphic Printing, Inc.

First Edition

"Good stories have the power to save us . . . The best resource against the world's stupidity, meanness, and despair is telling the truth with all its ambiguity and complexity. We all can make a difference by simply sharing our own stories with real people in real times and places . . . Quilted together, these stories will shelter us all."

Mary Pipher, author of *Reviving Ophelia* and *The Shelter of Each Other*

Dedication

*With deepest gratitude to all those who offered their
hearts and their stories on these pages.*

For my boys, Robert and Tyler.
For my teacher, Sri Eknath Easwaran,
and for Steve…whose lovingkindness
still lights my way.

–Lorrie

I dedicate this book to three people. The first is my
grandfather, Albert Merritt Ewert. He was truly a
Renaissance man–a minister, painter, composer,
organist, fly fisherman, naturalist, gardener, and
photographer. The second is Helen Anderson, a
remarkable woman who loved children and books.
Helen is one of my heroes. Her departure from this
island jump-started this work for me. Finally, I
dedicate this book to my wife, Nancy, who has spent
the last four years helping and supporting me
through this project.

–Greg

Contents

What is your reason for being? What brings vitality and importance to your life? When your time on this planet is done, what will you leave behind? These are the questions asked of thirty-two people living in a small, island community in the Pacific Northwest. Their answers offer a family album—a way to see ourselves in our own day-by-day process, living lives of richness, diversity, joy, confusion, struggle, and love.

In *The Healing Art of Storytelling*, Richard Stone writes that telling our story may be one of the most personal, intimate things we do. "Through storytelling…we reveal to others what is deepest in our hearts, in the process building bridges. The very act of sharing a story with another human being contradicts the extreme isolation that characterizes so many of our lives. As such, storytelling carries within it the seeds of community."

Kindred Spirits began for Greg Ewert twenty-five years ago. He dreamed of interviewing and photographing people, helping them share the essence of their own story. It was in 1995 that his dream took on the shape of this book. We met that autumn when my two boys and I moved to the island and my youngest son, Robert, enrolled in Greg's fifth-grade class. Greg and I connected around our mutual love of storytelling. He wanted to explore story through photography. I had been writing and presenting seminars in the corporate setting and was ready for more intimate writing. We decided to jump off the midlife high dive together. *Kindred Spirits* was born.

We chose our own community for the interviews. On this island of 1,800 people, hope is woven tightly into the fabric of daily life. People here have found a way to hold fast to the belief that, both individually and as a community, they make a difference. As Kathy Keller, one long-time resident, told me, "Caring is something we live by here. We expect understanding and acceptance from each other."

Our goal was to talk with a cross section of people. We are a rich gumbo: mothers, fathers, farmers, store owners, computer engineers, stonemasons, corporate executives who commute to the mainland, housecleaners with college degrees, retirees, contractors, people getting by on food stamps, artists, and young people of every stripe. We tried for a balance of age, gender, temperament, and occupation. What we discovered along the way is that every person's story holds truth and blessing. It wasn't a matter of selecting. If we could, we would have interviewed everyone. We conducted the first part of each interview together, usually staying two to three hours. I returned for a second visit to check quotes, clarify ideas, go a little deeper.

Over the span of four years, we did thirty-two interviews. They all appear here in a kind of delicious come-as-you-are-party. Some people are shy. Others are full of stories. Some have answers they are eager to share. Others are struggling with questions. But all have a willingness to be seen as they turn their hearts toward home.

A Longing For Connection

From the first interview, Greg and I felt something unexpected unfolding. Meeting in people's own homes, hearing them share their stories, we began to understand that the simple process of being asked, of being listened to, and of telling was itself transforming. Powerful energy is released when we put down our bags, face life's questions, and inhabit our own lives. While few of us remain on that inner frontier, visiting that sacred territory brings profound joy. Through sharing our stories we let it be known that we were here, our lives were led, and, in ways large or small, we mattered.

There is a longing inside us for contact, an ancient instinct calling for connection. We seek to validate our own experience by matching it with each other's. You know the feeling: that wonderful opening of the heart, when someone is brave enough to push the door past the customary crack and your life experience is acknowledged, reflected back in believing eyes. In that magical moment, you know you aren't the only one. Life becomes a little safer, because it is shared. Irene Claremont de Castillejo, in her book *Knowing Woman*, calls the experience "meeting." She speaks of it as an actual vibration occurring between people.

How meeting occurs, like love itself, is a mystery. The alchemy of its arrival refuses to be reduced to mere knowledge, but that doesn't keep us from knowing when it arrives.

A quickening, a lightness, a skittery excitement, a current of alternating joy sets up—and for a flicker of time we are more alive. Sharing our stories is one of the most powerful ways we meet.

My friend Martha, ninety-one, died recently after leading a full and independent life. She lived life so lightly that her passing left hardly a trace—no car, no will, just her books, a small bank account, a few personal belongings, and her parakeet, Cody. As was Martha's wish, after her death her things were passed along to others. Last week at the bank, Jill stopped to tell me how much she enjoys wearing Martha's white cardigan. She said that each time she puts her hand in the pocket a little memory comes back. "It feels so good putting her sweater on. I like remembering her." It reminded me that our stories outlive us. More than her sweater, it's Martha's story that keeps Jill warm.

In addition to the interviews, you'll find eight vignettes here—my own stories of making the quantum leap from city life to island life and finding the healing heartbeat of community. While I try to write from a place of balance, I admit to having a newcomer's zeal. There are communities in this country where life, despite its natural cycles of happiness and unhappiness, sanity and insanity, is abundant and gracious…and this is one of them.

From my first visit, the island began working its magic on me. Like a new planet in my hustle-bustle universe, it applied steady gravity, slowing me down, pulling me into its orbit. Maybe it was the long, lazy, ferryboat ride, or looking out at all that bottle-green water gliding past, but when I arrived, something changed. I was on island time, a kinder calibration than the speeded-up, get-everywhere-fast lane I knew.

Of course island life isn't for everyone. Visitors, delighted by our connectedness, are often startled by the simplicity of our choices. We have no mall or movie theater. There's no daily newspaper delivery (though you can get a paper if you drive to the ferry landing after 7 a.m.). We have a medical clinic, but no hospital. Hitchhiking is still normal transportation for local teenagers. The pharmacy and gas station close on Sundays. Nothing stays open twenty-four hours except the doors of the churches. There are no stoplights. We don't have an actual town, but call the little cluster of stores and restaurants in the center of the island "the village." Our three deputies go by their first names. Many people choose not to own a television. The ferries, which deliver everything from milk to mail, occasionally break down or are canceled by rough seas. A few winters ago, we went three days with no service at all.

We do have potlucks and concerts, barn dances and art galleries, a great library and theater productions well worth waiting for. Our bakery has been written up in the *New York Times*. People commute two hours from the city just to eat dinner in the Bay Cafe. We also have most of the troubles found everywhere: young teens becoming mothers and fathers, accessible drugs, family violence, lonely elderly, suicide, bored teenagers, a severe shortage of well-paying jobs, and a shrinking supply of affordable housing. What may be different is that those issues, large as they loom, don't often feel bigger than we are.

Reason for Hope

The feeling of connection spoken of in these pages is not unique to this island. It exists naturally in thousands of smaller towns all across the country. Examples abound in urban areas too, where people work hard to create and nurture new visions of vibrant community. This island is simply one example in a country hungry for encouragement. Let's pray for a sea change of belief that community is available to us all.

We hope you'll enjoy meeting these people. Look into their eyes. Hear their words with your heart. Our heritage of connecting through story is worth reclaiming. In the Sioux nation there is a traditional greeting, "mitakuye oyasin," meaning "we are all related." May we each find ways to remember, in the unfolding of these stories…and our own…that we are all kindred spirits.

Lorrie Harrison
September, 2000

Kindred Spirits

Emma Ewert

When you get older you forget about fairies. Maybe you can't see them *anymore so you say they don't exist. I know they do.*

Emma is sprawled out on the blue-painted floor of her art room coloring a poster she has drawn today. Right now she's choosing a color for the star-nosed mole.

Star-nosed mole…is that imaginary or real? I ask. She giggles, nonplussed by my lack of basic information. "It's real!" (Lots of exclamation points in this child's voice.) "I read about them in *Ranger Rick.* Don't you just LOVE moles and mice?!"

She has drawn a poster for me to color too, Mouse in the Sun. A big mouse in trousers waits on the page. She passes the box of crayons my way. I hesitate. As the artist here, Emma, how do you see this colored? Can you give me some idea of what you'd like? "Oh no!!" More giggles, and exclamation points. "YOU get to decide. ANY way is a good way. It's not my poster now. It's YOURS! Don't you think it's just fun to CHOOSE?!"

Emma is flowers today, head to toe. She dressed herself in a sunny shirt with bright little buds. Her leggings are a different palate altogether–bold splashes in blues, orange, and red. And on her feet, new Christmas socks, flowers again. "Almost never-ending flowers!" She makes it like a song. Three gardens growing on one little girl.

I decide to abandon the child-size questions I brought along for this seven-year-old. What is the best part of being alive, Emma? "That is a hard question for me. Maybe how much love I get. I like it how much love I get. It is so fun to be with the people I love. It's good when I get to be with them ALONE. Like being with my mom or with my dad.

"I'm just thinking that the childhood part in life is so short. It just seems short because you have such fun. Then comes the part when you're serious."

Her favorite book is *Charlotte's Web.* "That book wasn't really about spiders at all. It was about love and friendship."

We move to the topic of being the big sister. "It's fun and not fun," Emma says. "It's fun because you get the hand-me-downs first. Well, not always, but usually. And also it's fun because you get to hold your baby sisters. I got to hold Lilly AND Clara! But also…you CAN get bit!

"My favorite part of living here is how much nature there is. I like how you can see the moon so good. In cities, sometimes the buildings cover up the moon. I was just looking, and I can see the whole moon and its shadow."

What's the best part of being Emma? "I just like how fast I can learn. It makes me feel like I'm good at learning and that makes me BE good at learning! Well, you see, I'm a Taurus. Sometimes it's really hard to do something, but I never give up. I can DO it. Sometimes it takes a long time,

Emma Ewert

sometimes it's easy–like in tap. Tap dancing is one of my Best Skills.

"The one thing I do think is everyone is special in the same way and in different ways. Everyone is special just because they are the person THEY are. Like I may be special because I like to make things up and have a big imagination. And I may be special because I like myself.

"Sometimes I'm so shy. Sometimes I can talk so much I can't even stop! When I was three, I was the quietest I've ever been. I was just staring at the moon for about three hours. I don't think I'll EVER be that quiet again until I'm a grandma or something.

"I have no idea what I want to be when I grow up. I have so many choices. I could be ANYTHING! I am just going to think later. I'm probably going to be lots of things. When I'm a teenager I might be a gymnast, maybe in the Olympics if I get good enough. I'm pretty good at cartwheels right now.

"I like to be outside a lot. I really need to be outside. I just love to be in the forest, sitting. Sometimes I think about what I read in *Rami's Book* about meeting an angel or a gnome. And sometimes I just try that in the forest. I see an angel, or I feel it, just for a little bit. It's neat because most

people don't think fairies or angels are even around. I can PROVE angels are around. I see a flash of golden wings. I know it can be a fairy, it HAS to be a fairy. When you get older you forget about fairies. Maybe you can't see them anymore so you say they don't exist. I know they do. I've seen them and that proves it!

"I've thought about what I think the heart of life is: you always come back, but not always in the very same way. Like if you're a kid and you kill slugs until you're a grownup, then you'll come back as a slug. But if you stop, then you won't come back as a slug; then you get to choose the family you want when you come back. And this is the other part: you'll find a family that wants you too. You know that song, 'The Circle of Life'? It's like you keep having life, like a circle. A circle that would never end.

"I know something I was just thinking about when I was looking at the moon. If I could know anything on earth, I'd choose to know how the moon lights up at night! I think it is hot lava coming out, lighting it up, that's what I'm thinking. And no hot lava comes out on the nights we can't see the moon."

Lisa Geddes

It's one of those wiggle-your-toes-in-the-grass days, a day of butterflies in the garden and first blackberries fat and juicy on the vine. I sit on Lisa's porch waiting for our interview, the sun melting me like a pat of yellow butter. Up in the woods a breeze brushes through a wind chime. The music dances out of the trees, over the grass, behind the bees.

How will it be, meeting Lisa on this day? Her husband, Hugh, forty-nine, died just three months ago after an eight-month struggle with a brain tumor. Their children are so young: Elsa, just two; Emmett, five. Will sunshine and summer hold meaning for her?

We begin inside, Lisa, Elsa, and Emmett nestling together in a window seat off the main room. "I really welcome talking," Lisa says. "I am aware when some people politely avoid the subject, but in fact it's helpful to talk. I need to tell my story over and over. I learn a lot through the retelling, seeing how it changes slightly sometimes. I am lucky that I have friends who want to hear it.

"The children and I just returned from a trip to Oregon, where Hugh and I met. I had a strong need to run my fingers through the threads of our life together. I wanted to go without expectations, to just follow the pull. My relationship with Hugh did not end when he died. The trip helped me understand that.

"People have been asking how my life is changing. I don't have the words for that right yet. I don't have words to describe how our relationship continues to evolve. But it is a feeling in me, a knowing.

"When Hugh got sick, I decided to just open. Open. Sometimes, of course, I did just the opposite. I would hold on. It was frightening. But when I'd grasp too tightly, I would lose the use of my hands. I would pry my fingers open regularly, trying to learn to trust. I read a piece in *The Sun* magazine which talked about each of us having an Old One, in addition to the much-talked-about inner child, inside. I think that's who I called on.

"One of the things Hugh said at our wedding was 'I want to grow old with you.' There are ways I think we did that. Certainly we experienced a lot in a short period of time. We

were married almost seven years. At times I attempt to make intellectual sense of his death. Sometimes there is a sense to it I can't even explain.

"There were tragic elements to this, but it hasn't all been tragedy. One day I had gone to the post office. I was coming out when all of a sudden I saw the trees full of blooms. Cherry blossoms! Plum blossoms! Someone I didn't know well came up to say how sorry she was about our tragedy. But in that moment I didn't feel tragic at all." Fingering the tag of her tea bag, Lisa looks into the cup. "There were a lot of times like that, when seemingly opposite feelings were just right there together."

Early in March, a scan showed that Hugh's tumor was growing. The doctor offered measures to give Hugh more time, but it was clear they wouldn't help him recover. Hugh and Lisa chose no more intervention. She talks about the day they made that decision. "It was a joyous moment for us. I felt like we had all the time in the world. Indeed, it was just a couple of months. I remember we could have a delicious time just taking a long, meandering walk to our outhouse. Often we would say we had enough time. Sometimes now I think we did. But it doesn't always feel that way. It goes back to trusting the time we did have together.

"Our community carried and astounded me. I got a lot from people coming. I remember early on I sort of kept this account, thinking how can I ever repay everyone? The meals

15

coming in each night month after month, all the help, the donations of money, anonymous gifts of all kinds. Sometime in there I decided to just receive. I saw how giving and receiving are somehow the same. I think maybe that was one of the biggest things I learned, that receiving was a gift I could give.

"I have learned so much from all of this, but it's hard to make it all tidy…" Lisa's voice drifts into comfortable silence. The children shift their drowsy bodies, cuddling closer. "There are many things I think I knew up here, but now they've moved here." She moves her hand to her heart. "I didn't know the depth of my own laughter or my tears. I found the greatest, deepest laugh sometimes followed the hardest times, and that made perfect sense."

Have your thoughts about death changed?

"Hmmm, they have. I'd always wondered where *do* we go? If we're going to cease to be, what's that all about? Watching Hugh, it became very clear to me that he wasn't going to just go 'poof.' I'm reluctant to use words here. I love the mystery of it. I don't want to define it too much. I remember a very important time when Hugh and I were laying in bed, feeling swallowed in our pain. I remember stepping out of the room, the house, the islands. My God, we were just these little specks. It's a tool I used, a coping mechanism. I don't know what I'd call it, but it's about

having a different perspective, seeing our lives from another vantage point."

It's been a long visit for the children. We make plans to meet again.

Returning in a week, I find Lisa under her van with only her feet poking out. She's changing the oil. Elsa naps inside in her car seat. "This is me apart from Hugh," Lisa says, scooting out, slapping off the dust. "I'm in the midst of change, reintegrating some of the roles I comfortably handed to Hugh when we got together. Today I'm feeling mad at him because he's not here to help. I find myself feeling very much alone. I think I believed I had some kind of ownership of the future. But life holds many unexpected surprises. I'm learning to greet them and welcome them." She stops. When she begins again, she chooses her words very carefully. "Well, the truth is…I don't always welcome them. Sometimes I feel raw and assaulted. But when I'm willing to sit with them, then I find I can usually make room. There's a poem by Rumi called 'The Guest House,' which has become a touchstone for me about this. Along with the surprisingly painful moments, there are surprisingly joyful ones, too. I hope I can live my life staying open to all of them."

Elsa awakens. Lisa lifts her out of her car seat and holds her close. We walk through the maples up to the house and settle on the porch. Emmett and a pal race up in their Viking helmets, check in, then gallop off into the woods.

"I realize that, as a wife and mother, I didn't always recognize my creativity. I was being the 'home person,' which included keeping track of the family details. Looking back I can see I designed that role for myself. I think it was just my own notion of what needed to be. In doing that, at times I would feel myself shutting down, feeling closed in, uncreative. But even then there's a lot happening. Over time I've come to see how the little, everyday parts of living can feed creativity. I think creativity comes out of the ordinary. Like when we are caring for our children—the pulling on, the pulling off, the buttoning and unbuttoning—these are the seeds from which creativity comes, real life.

"I found, through all of this, I have come to claim myself as a singer. I don't know exactly where I'll go with it, but I see a lot of possibilities. When Hugh was first in the hospital I sang to get through it. I had in me a singer that shyness didn't even touch. I was singing for my life in some ways. I've always sung, but I've been shy. Now I understand music's medicine for me." The importance of her words shows in Lisa's radiant smile.

Can you talk more about what brings you joy?

"I love laughter. I welcome it. I love to walk. Sometimes I think it would be great to walk for days or months. I love to dance. I love to be outdoors." She lifts her eyes to the far tree line. Her gaze is steady. "It's amazing to me that I can be so moved just sitting in my own yard, right here under these maples."

The Guest House

This being human is a guest house.
Every morning a new arrival.

A joy, a depression, a meanness,
some momentary awareness comes
as an unexpected visitor.

Welcome and entertain them all!
Even if they're a crowd of sorrows,
who violently sweep your house
empty of its furniture,
still, treat each guest honorably.
He may be clearing you out
for some new delight.

The dark thought, the shame, the malice,
meet them at the door laughing,
and invite them in.

Be grateful for whoever comes,
because each has been sent
as a guide from beyond.

Jalal al-Din Rumi

Stewart, long and lanky, crosses his arms and leans back comfortably against his work- bench. "We're a forward- looking country. We move and throw out our furniture. Now we're even throwing away our heritage and myths. People don't want to look back, and it takes its toll. When we lose touch with our roots, then our models, anchors, and continuity are lost too. We're like a ship drifting, and there's plenty of rocks."

Tradition runs like a deep, wide river in this man. In high gear now, Stewart shifts to his own roots, Marshall Machine and Engineering Works, the family business since the 1890s. Here in his shop, beside his own tools, are

There's too much distance between us and our heritage. We've become

those of his father, grandfather, and great-grand-father. Stewart slides open the wooden drawer of his great-grandfather's tool box. "Look at this little gasket cutter," he says, the soft sounds of east Texas gentling his voice. "He probably made this tool himself around 1890 or so. Just take a look at the workmanship on this rosewood handle."

Most of the massive machinery in the shop, Stewart trucked here himself from the original family operation near Galveston. The newest of these machines was made about 1918. Huge leather belts, looping overhead, run the lathes, drill presses, and other machinery. The belts can last for one hundred years or more. "Even the new ones here were made before World War II. I do take them off every ten or fifteen years to oil them though." For a demonstration, Stewart flips a switch, starting the motors that drive the belts. The whole place roars to life–motors growling and thick belts spinning everywhere. It's mind-boggling. He laughs and shuts off the switch to quiet the racket.

For more than twenty years Stewart worked on the big boat engines. "I've worked on engines so big you could crawl in the cylinder and still have room to play a hand of cards. One engine was ten decks high. Hey, you could have fit a ferryboat sideways on the deck of that ship."

Like many people on the island, Stewart had to get creative to make a living here. He built a small foundry out back where he casts molten metal into hard-to-find replacement parts for marine engines. "I also cast builders' plaques and do some polished bronze work. I made some lion's head door knockers a little while back, borrowing the original off

an 1874 building in Victoria to reproduce it. It's cool, looks nice." He recently self-published a book on amateur foundry that is selling well on the Internet, and he repairs Macintosh computers for the locals.

"Anybody that moves here has to be pretty versatile. I've dug ditches, swung a hammer, carried stone, and been a carpenter's helper. That's what it can take to make it at first. We love living on this island. There is support here, people who will give you a leg up. It's a special place. It's a place for those of us that needed something different. It's a community of individuals. Everyone here has a story." There is a shy smile in his dark brown eyes as he continues. "It meant a lot to my wife Leta and me, once we finally got our place built, for our daughter Wendy to have her own bedroom. A home can be a tangible link with a person's heritage, to sit at your grandmother's old oak table, to see the family pictures on the wall. I remember thinking how neat it was to sit in the same chair my great-grandfather had.

"Kids today have a problem with identity, a loss of their individuality. They feel lost with no direction. I think when you lose touch with your heritage, with the forces that shaped you, that's when frustration sets in. You don't have a blueprint to draw from.

"We wonder why the U.S. is the most violent, frustrated country on the face of the earth. Well, there's no mystery about it; the kids just don't know who they are. I was one of those kids. One of the turning points in my life was going back to Britain, where my ancestors came from. I'd recommend a trip like that to any kid who wants to get his head screwed on straight. Save up. Go back to where your people

19

detached from who we are. It's just like you took a hatchet to a piece of rope.

came from. It turned me totally around. I was a pretty rough kid at eighteen. I took my trip between high school and college, and it settled me down. In that year I grew ten years. It made a grown man out of me. It showed me where I was from. I began to see who I really was. I was wandering around and saw old, abandoned buildings with weeds growing up–but there was my family name over the door. I found family gravestones going back to the 1600s. It made the hair stand up on the back of my neck. Suddenly I had my lineage handed to me from generations of Marshalls building engines. It was like opening a flood-gate.

"My family moved from England to Texas in the 1800s, but we always felt like outsiders. You can stay newcomers for three generations down there. My parents were upwardly mobile. They'd move to a new house every few years. That gave us no sense of place. My dad didn't even remember his own grandfather's name.

"I'd say it's how we handle our lives, our problems together, that is important. We're here to get through it until our number is up. The important thing is to not step on anyone else on the way. It's very subtle really. It's easy to step on others. People have to look at the big picture. They have to pull together. Hey, I've felt hatred. We all have it in us. We can be buttheads. It's an effort to sit on it, to stifle those dark parts in all of us. But it's the easy way out to give in to those feelings.

"Instead of killing each other, why don't we just scratch each other's backs and get through it? We're all gonna die. There's nothing we can do about it, not eating granola, not taking echinacea. Whether we've got one year or fifty, life is really about how we act with the people we're side by side with today."

Sue McCullough

Sue is out in her orchard when we pull up. "Hey! Over here. Come on back!" We walk through trees heavy with apples and plums. The grass, with the suns of a million dandelions blooming, smells like summer.

Sue's place is small and intimate. There's an old farmhouse and a second one-room building she is remodeling. She's doing most of the work herself. Today she hung the front door, giving it her artist's touch–a base coat of stain, another of paint, then a quick going-over with a hand sander. The door looks wonderful, as though it's been here forever. Sue shows the sauna she built a few months back, then we walk out to the garden.

"Gardening is definitely one of my passions!" Sue says she used to get revved up in the spring and go overboard with planting. When it came time for the harvest, she didn't have the energy to deal with all the food she'd grown. This year she planted mainly flowers.

An old cast-iron bathtub sits empty near the sweet peas. A tub? "The house only has a shower. Years ago I added this tub," she says, patting it like an old friend. I notice the charred remains of a fire underneath. Out here among the flowers and vegetables, Sue fills the tub with the hose, stokes a wood fire, and climbs in for a good long soak under the stars. It's a nice metaphor for this woman: fire and magic.

"Life is about attitude. That is so true. If your attitude is good, if you expect the best, it will come back to you. The kind of energy you put out is the kind you'll get back. No matter what you do, do it the best you can–doing dishes, doing your job, whatever." She's building up a head of steam. "Life should be fun! That's the whole thing. If you make it fun, it goes by better; you don't hurt so much."

What about that word "hurt"? Sue meets the question head on. "I mean physically and mentally. It's back to attitude. If your attitude is good, if there's humor in your life, then when there is pain, humor can be a balance. Sometimes I just focus on the pain, get into it, let the fog really roll in, and give it a good cry. But, on the other side of that, in the middle of the pain, it helps if you can feel that chuckle start way down inside, feel it start to build.

"My mom says if you get depressed, get busy. Do something. Step outside of your own itty-bitty space. Then things will come to you, things will get better. When I get really down, stressed, this magical thing happens for me with nature. I can almost count on it now. I can be really bitchy and crabby, just hating the world, and an owl will fly by. It's as if it's saying 'Do you think we can get this back together again, Sue?' It may be the totally wrong time of day for an owl to even be out, but still it will be there, like magic.

"My daughter once sent me a birthday card that said, 'You gave me the gift of magic. You gave me the gift of laughter. You taught me about joy.' There are so many people living here who have that. People on this island have room in their hearts for other people. One of the things that is so good about this place is if we act out of character here, there is forgiveness. It's about being respected and having that returned. It's something I'll treasure forever. But you work for that in a small community. It's really, really special. It's about integrity too. It all returns to treating people the way you want to be treated. Hey," she says, "I love this place. I've been trying to get elected mayor or homecoming queen here for over twenty years!"

Sue talks about what she calls "the wombness" of this community. "On one level, we're all isolated. You know

23

people, but you've never been to their houses. But if someone is in need, everyone is there. In this community there is a real safety net." She has been part of that safety net, especially for kids. Over the years, teens on the outs with their own parents have found their way to Sue's farmhouse. She'd give them a bed and make them call home. "They didn't have to tell their parents where they were, but they did have to tell them they were safe." The next morning she'd sit them down at her kitchen table. "Let's talk about the fifty-fifty part in relationships. What is your part in all of this?" she'd ask. "It's like I tell my son, 'You have to look at yourself in the mirror, not me. You'll work on being the kind of person you want to be for the rest of your life. It's never done.' Now you know one of my passions: kids. If I won the lottery, I'd go straight to the city to see what we could do for them."

She tells a little about her own childhood. "My mom was thirty when I was born; my dad, forty. They'd already lost two babies when my sister and I came along, so they were ready for us. I grew up adored! I thought everyone grew up that way. My mom is so cool. She's almost eighty now, Norwegian, very high energy. This woman totally lives what she believes. Mom used to give us these little talks before we were teenagers, effective little tools really. We called them 'The Series of Lectures by Maggie Davis on How-to-Be.' It was stuff like how human it is to feel less attractive than someone else, or how to go up to someone and start a conversation, or how to learn to step out of yourself and connect with people. She used to say, 'There's a lot of mistakes to be made; just don't make the same one twice. Mistakes are how we learn.'"

Sue lives life straight out, making it count. "This coming winter will be my first without my kids at home. It may be hard in ways. What I'll have to remember is warm water…and men who dance!" There's that smile again. It speaks of wonder, abundance, and deep joy. "I just love to dance. One of my friends says I'm the only woman she knows who dances while the band is tuning up!"

I love this place. I've been trying to get elected mayor or homecoming queen here for over twenty years!

Turning to Trust

Some people here say you can tell the tourists from the locals by who leaves their car keys dangling from the ignition when they shop at the market. Many of us don't lock anything, cars or houses. A realtor friend says that some islanders discover when they put their houses up for sale they don't even *own* a set of house keys. I know someone who left for two weeks last summer and taped a note on his front door: "On vacation. Come in. Please put the cat out when you leave."

"...but we all lose something far more precious than possessions each and every time we give in to fearing each other."

My brother Ron recently brought his children up from the city for a visit. After a full day, the cousins rolled out their sleeping bags side by side on the living room floor. Ron came downstairs to say good night to all the kids, then, walking to the sliding glass door, he flipped the little lever under the handle to secure the lock. Robert, my eleven-year-old son, watched. "What are you doing, Uncle Ron?" he asked. "Locking up." "Why?" came his question. Robert had never seen that door locked.

Grandma didn't lock her doors either. This was in Lewiston,

Idaho, in the late 1950s when, even though Wally and the Beave lived a safe life on TV, people in family neighborhoods like ours were beginning to lock up at night. I remember Mom explaining Grandma's viewpoint to me. "Locking up makes her feel afraid, like something bad will happen. She doesn't want to live with fear. She wants a feeling of safety, and for her that comes from *not* locking." "If they would steal from me, why then they must need it more than I do," Grandma told me later, as we sat out under her tree in metal lawn chairs. I loved the softness of her cotton dress covered with all those little flowers. I loved the softness of her life. It did feel safe there.

While plenty of us don't lock up, there are those who do. One view is that locking cars and houses protects kids from taking the first step of crime by removing temptation. "I never used to lock my car," says one islander, "but I had a camera stolen out of my front seat this summer. It makes me sad, but I usually lock up now."

Eknath Easwaran, a spiritual teacher from India living in the States for forty years, urges people not to accept the belief that fearing each other is a healthy way to live. "If you don't lock your doors, you may lose something sometime," he says, "but we all lose something far more precious than possessions each and every time we give in to fearing each other."

When television blasts those who tune in with a nightly dose of crime, and newspapers continue to headline grim

stories, it sends a low-grade current of angst coursing through our days, jittering our nerves and robbing our personal sense of safety. I feel it when I go to the city. I lock the car when I'm there, but am always aware of the discomfort it causes me. Something inside me shrivels up each time I choose to lock up. I want to carry a little of the island with me when I travel, acting on the belief that although fear is contagious, so is trust.

Healthy answers are hard to find. Accepting the current view, that we are safe only when we distrust each other, feels as distorted as believing that the Cleavers were a model family. What this island community has shown me is that fearing each other isn't a given. Hundreds of thousands of us in smaller communities all over this country are living with our doors unlocked and our keys in the ignition. For us, trusting others is a way of life. But it doesn't get much press.

The *New York Times* is open on the breakfast table, Sally's glasses on top of the page in a pool of winter sun. Beside the paper is a remarkable hand puppet. Sally knitted it years ago with wool from her own sheep. Spinning the yarn herself, she dyed the soft fibers with berries and plants from the island. The puppet's hair is thin now, the face worn, tender, sweet. How many children have hugged her? How many secrets has she been told? "Put your hand in the puppet!" says Sally. I do and feel like I have found my way into a Secret Garden.

In Sally's home, sky and sea seem to meet and dance right inside. The house speaks of her: baskets of hand-spun yarn, binoculars on the table, eagle feathers tucked around, family photos, the plump cat asleep on the window seat, plus books, books, and more books. Seed

me out of bed in the morning now. It twittles and twirls and talks.

catalogs and bulbs jumble into a cardboard box on the floor. A trio of stuffed animals cozy up in a child-size chair. Sheet music lies open on the piano–"Songs of the Sailor" and Mozart.

And now she's off to the kitchen fixing tea.

The only child of a New England couple, Sally studied physiology at Vassar. After graduating she took a position at MIT developing publicity films about radar for the military. "It was World War II and radar was new. It was what helped England survive the bombing," she says.

Sally and her sweetheart Sandy married in 1945 and moved to Seattle. A pioneer in pediatric surgery, Sandy began his practice at Children's Hospital. It's easy to imagine their life then. Six young children. The big, older house in the city. The kids grew, and soon it was backpacking trips, everyone learning to snow ski on the rope tow at Stevens Pass, car pools, scout troops, and sailing on the family boat. In winter, they flooded their backyard badminton court for neighborhood ice skating. "You could say I ran an ice rink. It was incredible! All the kids would troop in. We had a blast! That was where we spent some of our most memorable years." As their own children grew older, Sally and Sandy began taking in foreign students. "We didn't have enough children of our own!" Sally says with a throaty chuckle. "Yes, we had students from Brazil, France, Australia, and Yugoslavia come stay with us. I have this belief that if we just knew each other as people, we might be able to be friends and not up in arms against each other. But then, governments are one thing, and individuals are something else. I have a great resentment of this 'we/them' dichotomy. It's 'us.'"

In 1964, Sally and Sandy bought land on the island and started bringing the family for weekends and extended summer stays. It was Sally who especially relished island life. Here she could become the farmer that she loved being. When Sandy retired, they moved up full-time. Years later, the Yugoslavian student, who had stayed with them in the city, contacted them about her teenage son. She wanted to send him for a stay of his own. Arrangements were made. Andrija spent most of his seventeenth year on the island, away from his country's civil war. Living with Sally's daughter Molly's family, he played on the high school basketball team and was a member of the band.

Sally talks about the changes she's experienced in the year since Sandy died. "Life, you've got to live it! You can't just sit and pull out of everything; then it doesn't have any meaning. It's the eagle that pops me out of bed in the morning now. It twittles and twirls and talks. I enjoy it. For me there has always been this fascinating world out there. I have a curiosity about it all."

Our tea cups empty, it's time for Sally and her pup Angus to be off to their farm chores. They have more than fifteen goats, "mohair on the hoof," Sally explains. "Goats are more people-oriented than sheep. The big ones will smile at me." She slips into a work jacket and lets Angus out the door first. "I have to get some hay loaded here," she says. Together they head for her blue Dakota pickup. "It's ridiculous really. Angus and I need our critters to keep us out of the bars, I guess. As long as we can, we'll do it."

Jeremy Snapp

We begin at Ship Supply, Jeremy's newest venture. The place is due to open in about a month. Jeremy tells about renovating the old building, matching the molding on the tall sash windows, pine-tarring the board floor. Settling into a reclaimed leather armchair in the little back room, he cradles a paper cup in his hands and, blowing lightly, brings up steam from the black coffee.

"I'm a preservationist and, within that, an artist. I've looked at myself as an artist all my life. I want to say that. I'm not trying to put myself in any particular box. I've always

The thing is, you can always build a new boat, but you only

thought of my work as my art. Even when I'm building a new boat, I consider it preservation, preserving the art of boat building. I've been building boats since I was a kid. I built my first when I was twelve. It was an eight-foot rowboat, eight feet because that was the length of a sheet of plywood.

"This 1910 building was another thing." Jeremy lifts the hand with the coffee cup. "Look at this old-growth cedar shiplap. The place had so many beautiful, old-style characteristics. They were going to burn it down! I didn't want that to happen, so we moved it here to the village.

"I've acquired some vessels to restore and use, others to preserve. These things sort of have a way of presenting themselves. I feel a little better when I do this work. It's something worthwhile. Old boats are a little piece of history, but the thing is, when they're gone, they're gone forever. I look at this stuff coming my way for a while; then it's time to pass it on."

Along with boats, it's being on the water that's important to Jeremy. Later we meet at his house. "Let's go down to my summer living room," he says, grabbing a wide-brim straw hat from a hook by the door. Walking through the trees to a secluded community beach, we stop where the woods thin out. "This is one of my favorite spots. Mainly I come here in the afternoon and evening." A picnic table sits in a little clearing just above the water line. Grass grows past the bench tops. A circle of stones marks the memory of a campfire.

"Have a seat," he says. Settling against a mossy log, he stretches out and looks at the evening water. It's one of those soft, first nights of summer. Light from the dropping sun shines through the brim of Jeremy's hat, casting a crosshatch of shadow over his eyes, picking up the red in his beard.

I jump right in: Why do we live? Why do we die?

"Why is there air? Why do we breathe?" he volleys back, chuckling. "I don't have that hangup so much, the need to answer to all those questions. I'm comfortable breathing. If breathing is what we have to do, then breathe.

"There's a little bit of truth in everything, don't you think?" The philosopher in this man is showing up and having fun. He picks a little flower from the weeds and twirls it between his thumb and fingers. "The deal is, we're all a little crazy. The whole issue is how much craziness is acceptable and how much is considered crazy. That's the

have one chance to save an old one. I think you better look to the past.

Jeremy Snapp

issue for us as individuals, trying to fit in. Some of us try to fit in more than others. I always felt like I was just supposed to be here." Jeremy stops, as if he just heard his words replayed. "Now, I don't usually talk about this stuff. You have to put this in context…"

It's a little awkward. These aren't grocery line topics. Maybe playing for a little time, we talk about the interview process itself. "You sort of want to put people at ease, or not much is going to come out of their soul," he says.

Wading back in: When are you happiest?

Jeremy laughs. "It's kind of unfair to try to pin a person down with that question." A pause. "Being home with my family here on the island. That's when I'm happiest. That's about it."

If you knew you would die in three months, what would you do, what changes would you make?

"I don't think I'd do anything very different. Maybe some little things, but I wouldn't move somewhere else or change my work, if that's what you're asking. I'm pretty satisfied doing what I'm doing. When I was a kid, I grew up a little too fast. Celia and I moved here because we wanted a wonderful spot to raise our kids. No, I'd stay right here."

The family's old golden retriever wanders slowly up from the beach, carefully navigating the path. "Whew, you smell like low tide, KD! Have you been clamming?" The dog shakes, spraying saltwater everywhere. Jeremy doesn't even try to avoid the wet. "Come on," he pats the grass beside him, "sit by me."

As we talk, the sky pinks up, the water calms, a ferry glides silently by.

"I spent a lot of time with my grandparents. My grandpa was kind of a gruff guy. He didn't have a lot of patience with kids. The rule was, come in his shop but keep your hands in your pockets. He was involved in the things I was interested in, so I tagged along. He tolerated me because I was interested, but he encouraged me too."

A breeze picks up over the water. Suddenly the air feels like night. We walk past the house to Jeremy's boat shop, his first business here on the island. "Yeah, this guy in a white shirt and a skinny tie came out here once to inspect the place. He said to be a boatbuilder I needed a sign and an office. Well," he says with a wry smile, "at least I have my sign." He points over the doorway: Upright Boatworks.

Going inside, Jeremy shows his finish work on a new fifteen-foot lapstrake skiff. "I think it's my thirty-seventh boat. It may be my last, I don't know. The thing is, you can always build a new boat, but you only have one chance to save an old one. I think you better look to the past. It's important." He talks about taking on apprentices. "I've had quite a few. I like passing on the skill, the knowledge. Generally people just look me up and stay for a while, a few years, as long as they like."

The shop, actually three connected buildings and sheds, is jammed with stuff. Relics, remakes, remarkable stuff: the skiff, a 1936 Pontiac, an Argentine riding saddle, wooden nail kegs, a ship's wheel, a rack of old flannel shirts, hand tools, a huge band saw, a dinghy, a spittoon. Jeremy leans against a post, stroking his beard. "I wind up with a lot of stuff no one else wants to deal with. I guess you could say there's a desire in me to not let old things die."

Daffodil and hyacinth bulbs in clear glass vases sit in the windowsills at Julie's house. Their brown roots tangle down into the water, their green sprouts reach up for winter sunlight.

An old family cradle, wearing a fresh coat of aqua paint, waits in the living room. And there's Julie…soft and expectant, two weeks from when her son is due to be born.

Candles fill this house. There is something special about a daytime house with candles burning. It's subtle, the generosity their light brings. Their flames soften the corners of life, slow things down. Candles don't burn in busy, hectic homes. "There are armfuls of light in candles, good light and warmth," says Julie.

As we sit and talk, Julie's hands return again and again to the fullness of her belly. Moving to the place where the baby is kicking, they gently stroke, caress. It's clear this mother-to-be is mothering now, already finding ways to comfort her child.

"This whole experience of pregnancy has been about surrender. It's something totally new for me. It took us six years to conceive this baby. I'm learning to trust something completely unknown. It's trusting that the universe is going to let me have this baby, keep this baby, that this baby won't go away. And trusting that my body knows things I'm not aware of on a conscious level, the wonderment of growing a baby! I feel very powerful, my body knowing how to do everything necessary for a human being to grow.

"I've enjoyed each part of this pregnancy from the first heartbeat, the first wiggle. I decided from the start to let the wisdom of my body and my baby guide everything. I'm happy to have my body blossom, grow, get huge like this.

Dennis has been totally wonderful–a true partner in this adventure. We've had a lot of family support too. It's been a great experience, one of the favorite times in my life."

We go upstairs to the nursery with its nubby white carpet, the alphabet quilt behind the changing table, the whisper of yellow paint softening the walls. Through the skylight, morning almost tiptoes in. Shhh! A baby will soon be sleeping here. Julie tells about friends who lent the rocker, brought the crib, and made the wooden footstool.

Dennis and Julie are relative newcomers here. They bought their land eight years ago and began building a few years later. In 1996 Julie moved to Seattle to complete her master's degree in education and get her teaching certification. For that year, she commuted home to the island on weekends.

"I think the blessings of this island are immense. It's about community, about how people reach out to others. It happens over and over again here. The blessings are about people being sincere, generous. It has affected us deeply. We've learned great lessons. Dennis and I have experienced our own changes because of the way we have been treated. The kindness and generosity we've experienced remind us to come from that place, too. It becomes this wonderful dance of giving and receiving. I think as human beings we hunger for that contact, that interplay with each other. We hunger to share, to exchange ideas, to relate on a deeper level.

"For me the meaning of life unfolds day to day. It's elastic, it doesn't stay the same. As we get new information, it changes. When I look closely at the people dear to me, I see the spirit of what makes each of us different, that bit of life, that bit of light, that makes us unique. I suppose that's entwined for me with having a child, the struggles, the dreams, the excitement of learning that I would like to share with those I love.

"The older I get, the less I know. It's the questions that are growing in me. I've been looking, reading, listening. I don't know that I'm looking for answers so much as for more understanding. It's hard to sit still and look, though. It's much more comfortable to let yourself be so busy that you don't have time to explore, to ask the important questions about your life."

There is a softness in Julie that is more than her pregnancy. It shows in the calmness, the steadiness she projects when she talks about her own feelings of unsteadiness. "I am working towards having that constant mindfulness. It's about letting go. Letting go of our preconceptions, letting go of whatever you'd call non-movement, letting go of being stuck. Experience is about moving, shifting. Being uncomfortable is a necessary part of that transition. I find myself yearning for the lessons of letting go. It's really hard. I know intellectually it's essential," she laughs, "but it can be so uncomfortable!" Julie's laughter has a bubbling-up to it, an extra breath in there somewhere. It sounds like joy ringing.

Born in Ankara, Turkey, into an Air Force family, Julie attended twelve different schools before high school graduation. She says the experience taught her appreciation of differences and gave her a willingness to risk change. "I think it's easier to go through new experiences than we realize. I can say to myself, 'This is just an experience, not a commitment. It's something to try, to taste.' Trying something new, like a move or a career change, doesn't have to be a ten-year thing. It may simply be something to try and see what happens.

"For me life is about journey, process, experience. And it's about struggle, learning, and growing." Julie takes her time before going on. "I think not inviting change is about fear. Sometimes I think what keeps us from moving toward change is wanting to know in advance that things will be perfect, that it will be the 'right' move. It's so rare when we can have that. I don't think we ever really can. So it becomes a leap of faith to invite change into our lives.

"The time we have to do things in life is finite. I don't want to miss those opportunities. We want to pass that on to our son, the idea that life is about experiences. We want to help him find and nurture what he wants from life. It has a lot to do with paying attention. Being there. Being present in your child's life. Dennis and I really look forward to that. Becoming parents feels a lot like having the opportunity to heal pieces of our own childhoods too.

"The experience of loving a child is so huge to me now. Having the opportunity to love and share in a child's life is just the biggest, the best thing. I can feel it. I know it will be the truth for me. I'm overwhelmed with feeling fortunate and blessed that we get to do this."

Her hazel eyes turn to gaze out the window and across the fields. In the quiet, I become aware again of the candlelight and comfort here. "I suppose if you asked the meaning of life," Julie says, "it would be to enjoy, embrace, and cherish love…both the giving and the receiving. That's the richest part of life for me."

When I look closely at the people dear to me, I see the spirit of what makes each of us different, that bit of life, that bit of light, that makes us unique.

Huck Phillips

Some islanders call taking the ferry to the mainland "going to America." It can feel that way too, as if much more than water lies between us and the rest of the country. When I visited Florida recently, friends at a casual dinner party asked about the progress of this book. "I'm working on an interview with a man who chooses to live in a bus," I said. "A bus?" someone asked. There was dead air. Looking around the table at these wonderful, longtime friends, I saw a total lack of understanding.

The fact is, more than a handful of islanders choose bus life for their home life. Decent, moderate housing is in very short supply here. Jobs that pay a living wage are equally hard to come by. Many people rely on ingenuity to make island life work.

Huck Phillips, twenty-seven, is one. Since he got his B.A. in organic farming in 1994 from The Evergreen State College, he's been working a choice piece of land on a friend's farm and living in a converted 1955 Chevy school bus. In the winter anyway. By early June each year, he moves to his "summer home," a lodge-pole, canvas tipi.

"There can be a lot of tourists and slow drive-bys," Huck says, smiling. "I'm kinda tucked back here in the trees off the main road. Sometimes people stop to take a look, maybe even snap a photo. It doesn't bother me much…they're just curious. Around here, there are a lot of people living in

39

Hey, if I were subjected to flush toilets again, I don't know

trailers and mobile homes, but I think people are baffled by the bus."

Sitting at his kitchen table with his little wood stove kicking out the perfect heat, Huck talks about his choice. "Some people call bus living simple living; others call it sane living. To me there's no one way to live. Choosing a bus was partly about aesthetics. A bus has character; it feels more like a cabin than a trailer. Economics was part of it too. It's a way for me to have some home security without going into debt. If I do eventually have my own land and a house, I could use this for guest space or a studio. This bus cost $5,000 totally remodeled and highway safe." His dark eyes twinkle. "Well, maybe that's an overstatement, 'highway safe.' It made it here anyway!"

With a welcome mat out front, handmade wooden front door, stained-glass window up top, new parquet floors, covered back porch, and plenty of light pouring in those big bus windows, the place is both snug and sweet. A wire basket holding a few onions hangs in the trim little kitchen. Huck's only auxiliary piece of furniture, a bookcase, over-flows with books. A rope ladder with wooden rungs leads "upstairs" through a two-by-three-foot opening in the original roof to a cedar-paneled bedroom loft. Skylights and big windows bring the stars in close.

While the bus seats are long gone and the back has seen a total remodel, the driver's area remains just as it was in the 1950s. "Hey, look at this ashtray by the driver's seat," says Huck. "Can't you just see the bus driver, with a cigarette in

his hand, waving hello to the little kids climbing on board carrying their lunchboxes?"

Indoor power comes from a solar panel on the roof. It generates enough juice to meet Huck's needs: a CD player and reading lights. Twice a week he hauls water in six-gallon jugs from a friend's well. The shower is a gravity-feed job he rigged up on the porch using a green bucket for the water reservoir and a garden sprinkler for the shower-head. "It works out pretty good. I heat the water here on my stove first." His outhouse is in a little stand of firs nearby.

How does he handle the lack of indoor plumbing? "I kinda like the experience of going outside, being in the elements. Even in winter you just throw on a coat and head out there. It's only been a problem when I've been sick or if it's storming. Hey, if I were subjected to flush toilets again, I don't know if I could handle it!"

Huck traveled and lived in Central America before coming to the island. "In some ways, being there may have been part of my decision to live this way now. Many people live in smaller dwellings there, closer to the land.

"Sometimes I think about my impact on resources by living simply. It makes me wonder, what if a small percent-age of our population chose a simple, low-impact lifestyle for even a few years? Think what that might translate to in terms of conserving resources and impacting people's thinking about what we use. Even if I happen to live in a conventional situation later on, and have way more than I

if I could handle it!

need, I'm sure this experience will permanently affect the way I relate to water and power usage."

Sitting cross-legged in the sunny window seat, hands resting on his bare, brown feet, Huck continues. "I've been here several years now, and I really appreciate having this place. While my lifestyle might be seen as extremely simple or rustic to the average American, I'm not assuming all people have the choice to live like this, or the privilege to choose their lifestyle. I'm guessing that compared to most people on the planet, my life is one of abundance."

Huck's simple choices extend to his work. "I've found myself in the role of being a farmer. I make my living growing vegetables and berries and sell them to the store, to restaurants, and at our farmers' market."

For the last two years, he volunteered to run a summer program called The Learning Food Garden, helping young people make their own connections to the land. "I have an interest in working with kids of all ages. A few years ago, several community members and I wanted to see kids get involved in agriculture, to learn at a young age about growing organic food. It's easy to get pretty disconnected from that process. As a result, we developed this program where a group of twelve- and thirteen-year-olds help out on the farm. Depending on what's happening in the fields, they plant, harvest, weed, mulch, and help sell the produce. I take them on a three-day camping trip at the end of the summer. We cook food we grew ourselves, and that's fun.

"One reason I was drawn to this community," Huck continues, "was the feeling of respect and acceptance people have for each other here. It feels like a sane and natural way to live. I think it's pretty different from what's generally going on these days. What disturbs me greatly is that there is a lot of fear in our culture. Fear in general and fear of each other. Fear is a natural part of the human experience, but I'm not convinced that the degree we find ourselves fearing each other is natural. I don't think it fits in with our potential."

Any final thoughts, postscripts on the bus life, comments for people out there in America?

"To me there's nothing incredibly unique or extraordinary about living like this," Huck says. "I don't have a constant awareness of how funky it is. After a time, living here becomes normal, just like any other lifestyle. I guess for some of us the camping trip never ended!"

41

A Mother's Day

It was a great Mother's Day. After a potluck brunch with three of our favorite families, my boys and I joined our friends out in the horse field to top off the day with a few innings of softball. Everyone got in on the action. A six-year-old coached runners at third, my teenage son caught behind home plate, and our first-time pitcher got tips from a dad who played pro ball for the California Angels. I held down second base with Lilly, age four. One father, smacking a long one out to center, carried his littlest ones around the bases, one under each arm.

When the game wound down, we said our goodbyes. For our family it was time for our Sunday-afternoon routine …homework and housework.

Pushing the Hoover back and forth, trying to get up all the dog hair, I heard a knock at the sliding glass door.

Randy is one of the people I wave to, might even say hello to if we were beside each other in the grocery line, but we've never had a conversation. Probably in his mid-thirties, he shares a small place in the woods nearby with a woman friend. He stood at the door in his plaid shirt and jeans, a little smile playing under his wild, bushy beard.

I opened the door. "These are for you," he said, shyly holding out a bouquet of white lilacs, magenta rhododen-dron, and soft, pink honeysuckle. "Happy Mother's Day."

Wonder welled up inside me. The bouquet was beautiful! Confusion came next. A man I hardly knew bringing me

flowers for Mother's Day? I gathered up my courage. If he could bring the flowers, I could ask him about it. "Mother's Day is my favorite holiday," he told me. "I fill the back of my pickup with flowers and deliver them all over the island. I missed you when I came last year, but I left a little bunch here by your door."

"I remember," I said, a light going on. "Thank you. Twice." It was my turn to feel shy. "But how do you choose who to give to?"

"Some are mothers or grandmothers I know, some I've just heard about. In your case, I know your boy Tyler. He's a really cool kid." Randy smiled that little smile again. There was an easy pause. "Well, goodbye," he said. Then he gave me a hug. It was so unexpected, that hug…big, warm, full of kindness. A hug with a long, comfortable breath inside of it.

The bouquet sits in a vase on my writing table. I think the flowers were picked from local gardens and woods, maybe even the roadside. Their blooms carry the blessing of sun, wind, earth, and soft rain falling. Some flowers look pretty, but have no fragrance. These fill my room with tender perfume.

"There were two phone systems back then—a party line we called the farmers' phone and the long-distance line for calling off the island. Our ring was one long and two shorts. Uncle Joe and Aunt Susie Gallanger's was three shorts. Daddy wouldn't let us listen in on the party line, but our cousins sure did. We'd get to school and they'd tell us everything that was going on!"

Frances Kring, born here in 1917, sits at the kitchen table reminiscing about her growing-up years.

"We had a horse and buggy and did our shopping down at Port Stanley. You know the lagoon? Why, that second little house down there was our grocery store back then. There was a long dock out into the bay. A steamer boat, the *Alvareen*, would come take us for a day trip to the mainland. They'd put down a gangplank and we'd walk right on board. I remember the cabin below deck. There were red plush seats!

"Where you lived decided where you'd go to church. It took a while to

Gerhart

get there by horse and buggy. Of course, when someone died, you'd go; it didn't matter which end of the island their church was on. I don't ever remember not going to church.

"There were ten or twelve of us in the first-grade class. My sister, cousins, and I walked two miles to the Port Stanley schoolhouse. I was just six and remember getting so tired walking that long ways.

"People used to visit a lot back and forth. Our family had a little place, just five rooms, but we could get twenty people in there anyway. We always had someone living with us. It was a good life. Once, during the Depression, a young man came and spent the winter. He and Daddy put hot and cold running water in the house. I thought that was great. But it was hard times too. Our days were spent trying to get ahead, and trying to catch up!"

Gerhart joins us from the other room. How are you? I ask, after introductions. "Still movin'," he answers, keeping his face straight. "Did you make coffee?" he asks Frances. She shakes her head. "I'll get it." He turns to the sink and fills a pot with tap water.

A few minutes later, he brings the fresh pot to the table. "Coffee?" he offers. I reach for the sugar bowl, adding a spoonful to my cup as he pours. "I thought you said you wanted *coffee*," he growls, but the twinkle in his eye gives him away.

They've lived together in this house for fifty-two years. The country kitchen is all comfort: the fire in the stove, the

little side room full of potted plants, the thermometer mounted next to the wall calendar. Family snapshots cover the fridge. Frances goes to the cupboard for cookies and brings six varieties arranged on a pink china plate.

Gerhart came to the island in 1932. "We had a couple or three bad years farming in South Dakota. My folks and Barney Goodrow's folks were close friends back there. Barney's dad had a church in New Underwood, but he preached in one-room schoolhouses too. Well, their family came out here and wrote back how everybody on the island had a pretty good orchard. My dad was doing a lot of gruntin' and groanin' about the hardships of our farm, and I guess he had the idea we needed an orchard to live on. So our family came too, lookin' for a place to get something to eat and get by. There was no money when we got here. I worked general all-around work, shockin' hay for ten dollars a month, if the farmer had enough to pay. You betcha it was hard times. I was eighteen years old."

He and Frances married in 1936. "Yep, she caught me," he says. They have three children, and seven grandchildren and great-grandchildren.

"Warm up your coffee?" Frances asks her husband. "Yeah, while you got it there." Gerhart holds out his cup.

"We farmed here for years," he continues, "grain mostly and pigs and cows. Then I was with the road department; roughly twenty-seven years is what they said it was when

45

Where you lived decided where you'd go to church. It took a while

they counted 'em up. A lot of the roads weren't even gravel back then. Some were only passable part of the year. They would go to bog. We couldn't use Dill Road at all in the winter. I really liked the work. It was a good job if you didn't let the politicians ride you into the mud. You might say we had a couple of #2 shovels and a wheelbarrow, compared to all the gear they got out there today."

Is there advice you'd like to pass along?

"No, not really. Of course if it was my grandkids I'd tell 'em to keep their noses clean!"

What has helped you along the way?

Gerhart leans back in his chair and crooks his cane over his thigh. Putting big hands palm to palm, he takes his time answering. "What has helped me along the way? Good neighbors, good friendly people to get along with. It's been over fifty years we've been neighbors with Barney and Marguerite. Now Frances," he says, "she's the kind of person who goes out and meets people by the dozen. She never has what you'd call a lonely moment. Not me. I don't mind meeting people, but from there it's hard for me to carry on a conversation."

Frances answers now. "I made up my mind once I wasn't going to let myself be unhappy. You know, for me it's been 'Do the best you can and things will work out.' I've had a good life. It's strange, isn't it though? You don't have any choice about coming or leaving this life, either one. As for the meaning behind it, I wish I knew. It goes by too fast."

The two pose for a photograph by the garden gate. Their dog comes up, weaseling his way into the shot. "Buster, go lay an egg then, damn ya!" Gerhart tries to shoo him off with his cane. The old pup stays put, tail thump-thumping the dirt.

From the garden, where dahlias grow the size of pie plates, we hear a little voice. "Hey, Grandma!" It's four-year-

old great-grandson Derekk. "Just a minute, honey. Be right there," Frances greets him. She turns back to her flowers. "They are all so pretty. I like taking a bouquet up to the cemetery. Mama loved the purple…"

She takes the little boy's hand, and we all cross the road to the barn. No one would take this woman for eighty-one. "Well, Dr. Dengler said I'd better come in for a physical before he retired. It had been eight years. You just can't worry about illness, I guess, and I haven't. I've just been really, really lucky. I hope I stay that way!"

In addition to their farm, Frances and Gerhart still have the family cabin down by the water. Frances keeps a second garden there in the summer. "It's a good food garden," says Gerhart. "She plants the whole damn thing. She works the whole damn thing. She weeds the whole damn thing, and I eat it all."

"Between that garden and the apple picking, we're down there four hours a day steady," adds Frances. "We have corn, beets, onion, carrots, a few zucchini, one pumpkin plant, lettuce, of course, and lots of good tomatoes this year. The crows pulled up my squash."

Back at the house, Frances pushes her sweater sleeves to the elbow and slips in between two big bushes by the porch steps. "Here, let me see if I can get you a hydrangea start." Bending low, she tugs hard to get a four-foot section free. She hands it to me, then claps the dirt off her hands. "Come on inside. Do you like bush beans? I've got some right here. Mom raised these, now let's see, that would be way back. I know they've been growing here on the island since 1905." She empties a handful of shiny speckled beans from a glass jar into a little paper bag and presents them to me with a smile.

It's almost dark. Gerhart stands. "Nice chattin' with ya. I gotta go feed my cows."

get there by horse and buggy.

Dwight Lewis

"Now this area here used to be a junkyard. Realtors on the island would make a detour so they wouldn't have to bring folks by. Then I bought it. Look at it now. I've parked it out." Dwight Lewis sweeps his sun-browned arm wide. The rolling acreage of Windsock Farms is lovely as a park. Looking at the cows grazing the emerald fields, it's hard to believe that only a few years back this property was scarred and ugly, the soil chewed up by heavy machinery, the land dotted with the rusty carcasses of discarded automobiles.

Standing in the sun, his blue corduroy baseball cap shading his eyes, Dwight smiles warmly and laughs freely, enjoying the chance to tell a good story. Gesturing with hands that have seen decades of serious, sixteen-hour days, he comes across as easygoing. Then something else finds its way into the conversation. "Controversy makes life interesting, that's my story," he says. "Tell me I can't do something, now that's what gets me going. I'm a little bit of a free spirit." He grins broadly, obviously enjoying the understatement. Dwight is known in this community as a rule-breaker. For him, fighting the system gives life its juice. But he's found that running fast and loose with rules can make people uncomfortable and angry. "I can't fit it into my schedule to get concerned about people getting up in arms about what I do." No apologies here. "I don't play by the rules, and when you don't, there are consequences.

"Some people have the image that I'm just out for the money, that money is all I'm interested in. I've spiffed up my image on this island. You can come up here to this part of my land and look at this beauty now, see what I've done. Stewardship is the name of the game for me." He mimes a kiss to his hand and gives himself an imaginary pat on the back. "I think now people might say, 'There has to be some good down deep in that Dwight Lewis fella that he cares about the land like that.' We mellow out with age. Just because people have a little tiff here and there doesn't mean they have to be enemies forever. You can't hold on to it."

His company, Windsock Farms & Excavation, offers services ranging from road building to septic pumping and backhoe work. "I see life as an unlimited opportunity. It's about how hard you want to work. I myself am an overachiever, basically a workaholic. The thing is, I'm either workin' or sleepin'. I get started and I just can't stop. It's projects I like."

Dwight's latest project is People's Park, another renegade deal. This time he illegally improved a piece of public property on the lake adjacent to his land. It had been a knot of blackberry brambles, a potential hazard for kids wanting

49

Dwight Lewis

to use the lake. After clearing, regrading, and grass-planting, he's made it a safe little spot, picnic benches and all. "The thing is, this land belongs to all of us. I think I got to their hearts a little bit. I think people are starting to see Dwight Lewis is out for a little more than making money. All this," he says, indicating the park, "is for someone else. It hits you right here to be able to give something back, especially for kids." Still, some neighbors take issue with his actions. "Sure, I irrigate out of the lake without a permit now," he says, addressing their concerns, "but the approvals will come through soon."

Clearly Dwight has his own strong code of ethics and plays by some rules. The question is, which ones? "I could never sit still in school, still can't," he says. He found more success in sports, playing linebacker for two years in junior college. Later came two short-lived marriages and a stint in the Army. "I was an E-1 when I went in, an E-1 when I came out. I hated the Army! Too many rules."

"I'd like to be frozen in time just where I am. I like where I'm situated. I don't want to go back to being thirty-five or forty-five. No. If I could, fifty-five is where I'd stay. It's a good time. You gotta smell the roses. I've worked for other people most of my life. Now I'm doing it for myself. It's fun! I'm working for the personal enjoyment now. It's my customers on the island who have helped get me where I am

today. As controversial as I am here, if I didn't do a good job for them, I'd have a problem. I'm not perfect, but I do try hard.

"I don't have close friends, no. I always found out you keep your distance from people. I don't want to be involved in their problems.

"My most important accomplishment? Staying married to Shirley for twenty years," he says not missing a beat. "Having her put up with me that long…that and being smart enough to hold on to her."

We move on to philosophy. Dwight likes the topic. "Where ARE we?" he asks. "You look up at the galaxies and just have to wonder how we're all connected to the universe. You gotta dream. It's just not going to happen if you don't. It's strange how we all have our different ways of going about life. I'm glad we're not all the same. The thing that does scare me is that kids today can't get a natural high. I get up at 5 o'clock, see the sun come up, look at my critters—it just psychs me up. It's about the beauty of the land, the lake, and stuff.

"How many people would give their left arm to live here? It's just beautiful. Whenever they chop me off in this life, it's okay. I've gone four hundred times past what I ever thought I was capable of achieving. It's been a real good life."

Controversy makes life interesting, that's my story. Tell me I can't d

mething, now that's what gets me going.

Mary La Porte

"I count none but sunny hours."

Quote on the sundial in Mary's garden.

It's hard to know where to start Mary's story. Do we begin with the five-year-old taking her first violin lesson at Seattle's prestigious Cornish School where "as a little girl, I remember my teacher's feet more than his face!"?

Or do we meet her during the Depression at her first job? She was Mary Jones then, single, sophisticated, talented, and very determined to make her living as a musician. A news clipping in her scrapbook shows her in a formal pose, part of a trio at Monticello College in Alton, Illinois. The caption reads: "Accomplished, sincere musicians express the devotion of this college to the ideal of music in the highest order." Mary laughs. "I wouldn't trade that wonderful time for anything. It was 1935. I worked for room and board, and I made $1,800 a year!"

She moved on to become director of the Pittsfield Community Music School in Massachusetts, but left the position during World War II. Determined to help support our troops overseas, Mary joined the USO. She was assigned, with a trio, to the South Pacific, to play for wounded GIs. Toward the end of the war, she was sent with a group of eight musicians to entertain Russian and American soldiers in Czechoslovakia.

Harris Goldman, friend for more than thirty-five years and a fellow musician, says, "Mary was, in her own right, a world-class musician. I'm not talking about Washington State or even the U.S., I'm talking the world. She not only played, she composed. You should have heard her! Such talent. Extraordinary. You should know that after she married, Mary chose to live in the shadow of her husband."

Mary and Lucien met in 1949. "My parents wanted to get me away from a cellist I was dating in Seattle. I went to New York and married a cellist!" She was thirty-nine at the time; Lucien, forty-nine. "I saw this little shrimp at a gathering," she laughs. "We got into an argument. That's how it all started!

"I am so very, very grateful that I met Lucien." A wistful sigh. "He gave me a combination of love and great music. We lived in the pleasure of making discoveries together. I respected this man who was a wonderful human being, who was bubbling with humor. I'm very glad to have had that experience."

It was Lucien's career with the world-renowned Paganini String Quartet that most influenced their life together. For twenty years they made their home in Los Angeles, where the quartet headquartered. Theirs was a rare lifestyle, travel-

53

ing regularly to Europe. Mary's career continued. Doing studio work for MGM in Hollywood, she played on soundtracks for *Psycho, Ben Hur, Dr. Zhivago,* and others. "Oh, I played on a lot of them," she says casually, as if this were something any of us might do. I comment on her extraordinary life. "No, no," she responds, "my life isn't extraordinary. You have to have curiosity, that's all. People are the ones who keep you going. You get fascinated with people. I have loads and loads of wonderful friends here. What I like is that so many of them are young people.

"When we moved here, I was unsure about what to do with the rest of my life. I thought I might want to teach, but realized I'd done enough. What I've been doing is making discoveries. I've had a great time getting acquainted with books and with my garden. The big discovery now is that I have an illness they don't seem able to assess. It's called leukemia and is quite a dramatic thing. There's not much of anything I can do. Illness has given me time for introspection. It's going to be interesting because it becomes a study of myself. My life has been in several directions. I divide it into everything before I met Lucien and everything after we met. This part, though, I don't find too exciting."

Mary responds to a question about life's meaning. "A question like that is like asking how high is up. You have to live a few years to have answers to any of that. I think those answers will come later on."

Like the saying on her sundial, Mary likes to count her sunny hours. "I'm not very vocal when it comes to talking about my feelings," she says. "You have picked me at a bad time. My husband died and my sister died. I've had too many things happen. I'm kind of mad at God right now …I'm not sure you want to put that in your story." It's as if she is sorry to say these things, as if life should be sunnier. But two deaths and cancer in the space of seven years are hard. They simply are.

Mary is feeling weak now. She goes down the stairs one step at a time, resting a few moments on the landing before tackling the second flight. It could be a difficult moment for this proud, independent woman, but she accepts the new limitation with grace. "It's like Rudyard Kipling might say in *The Just So Stories*: 'sometimes it's best to take things little by little.' You give a little here, you give a little there, and you hang on just the same." Mary smiles, then slowly walks down the rest of the stairs.

Bill Walker sits on the deck outside the bakery this summer morning. His bright, blue eyes telegraph enthusiasm. His smile is genuine, wide open. "I take people at face value," he says.

"In the Bible it says treat people how you want to be treated. I take that very seriously. A few minutes ago a young girl came up to use the pay phone, but she didn't have a quarter. Well, I just got up and gave her one. That's what I mean.

"I feel love is very important, showing love. Like it says in the Bible, 1 John, chapter four, it tells us to love one another. I think that's what the world needs. The hatred, violence, and prejudice of the world breaks my heart. If people could just get along…" His words trail off. "It's not my place to judge others, but I just feel that caring about people is a very big part of living."

Bill's CPR work is one way he shows that caring. Today he wears a red shirt with CPR printed in white block letters on the sleeve. He stresses he's not a professional, but has taken courses available to the public. "I enjoy helping people. I've got everything I need right here." He pats the blue canvas first-aid pouch on his belt. "I've got sterile pads for adults and special Band-Aids for the kids, Batman and Robin ones and dinosaurs ones too." His specialty is helping kids with cuts, scrapes, and bee stings.

"I really love this island; it's the best place to live. I've got a lot of friends here. I tell you, life is awesome, it's good. I'm a bachelor and live in a twenty-four-foot trailer on my sister's property. I don't have much, but I'm thankful for what I have. I wouldn't trade it. I'm not a rich man, but I'm not a poor man either. There are lots of people who have less than I do. I can say this, I'm rich in spirit, that's for sure.

"I love the Lord and He loves me. I'm a child of God and a Christian, and I'm not ashamed to say it. Lots of people are, but not me. I have a lot of love. It was Jesus who taught me how to love. Jesus keeps me going. I'm very honest about it. I think that's one reason people up here like me. They know I'm honest, they can trust me.

"Before I knew the Lord, I didn't have no love. I was a nasty person. I smoked a corncob pipe and did a lot of drinking. You used to see me walking with a big boom box on my shoulder. I wore big pants. I had a very bad temper. Ninety-nine percent of the time people didn't speak to me. I had a chip on my shoulder and they knew it. The Lord has totally changed me.

"I have a message for kids: Treat your parents with love and respect. Do what they tell you. You never know when they will be gone. My dad was killed in a car wreck two years ago, and my mom died of

Bill Walker

a heart attack when I was thirty-five. When my mom died, I felt like I lost everything. We were inseparable, just like Elvis and his mom, a very close family. My mom and dad were the strong ones. They taught me to be polite, to have respect for others. My dad taught me to treat ladies well. No one ever has the right to hit a woman. My mother always said, 'Remember, we will always love you.' My closest friend now is my sister. She is somebody I can always go and talk to if I have a problem. I understand her and she understands me. She's a very wise person.

"I look life right in the face and enjoy it," he continues. "A very important part of my life is that I celebrate life every day. I always try to bring a little more love and light back into the world, because the world needs it. In the evenings I read the Bible a lot. I'm in the book of Amos now. The Bible is my favorite book. I can nearly go back and tell you everything I've read in it. I like murder mysteries too, and old Westerns on TV. We've got a satellite dish on our property. My favorite shows are cartoons, especially *Scooby Doo*. I'm kind of a kid at heart. I like watching *The Flintstones* and *Quick Draw McGraw* with my nieces and nephews. They get so excited when I watch with them. Not many adults will watch cartoons with kids."

Bill is ready to be off. "I don't drive a car. Walking is the best part of my day," he says. "I meet people and greet them with a smile on my face. I can show them that life is great, don't worry, look forward to each day. Hey, the best transportation in the world is walking. After all, my last name is Walker! Sometimes I walk all over this island."

The gravel crunches under his strong, solid step as he sets off. "Hi. Hello! How are you today, sir?" he asks a stranger, not breaking stride. The man stops, surprised. He looks closely at Bill, and smiles back.

I'm not a rich man, but I'm not a poor man either. There are lots of people who have less than I do . . . I'm rich in spirit, that's for sure.

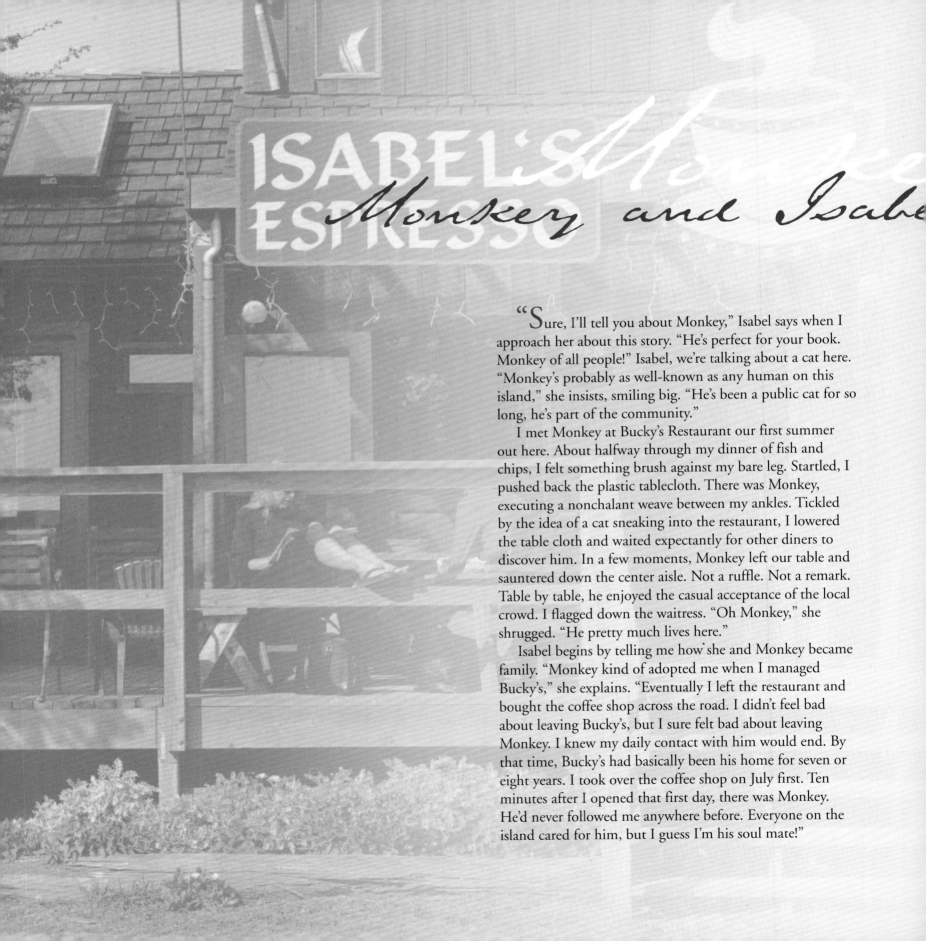

ISABEL'S Monkey
ESPRESSO
Monkey and Isabel

"Sure, I'll tell you about Monkey," Isabel says when I approach her about this story. "He's perfect for your book. Monkey of all people!" Isabel, we're talking about a cat here. "Monkey's probably as well-known as any human on this island," she insists, smiling big. "He's been a public cat for so long, he's part of the community."

I met Monkey at Bucky's Restaurant our first summer out here. About halfway through my dinner of fish and chips, I felt something brush against my bare leg. Startled, I pushed back the plastic tablecloth. There was Monkey, executing a nonchalant weave between my ankles. Tickled by the idea of a cat sneaking into the restaurant, I lowered the table cloth and waited expectantly for other diners to discover him. In a few moments, Monkey left our table and sauntered down the center aisle. Not a ruffle. Not a remark. Table by table, he enjoyed the casual acceptance of the local crowd. I flagged down the waitress. "Oh Monkey," she shrugged. "He pretty much lives here."

Isabel begins by telling me how she and Monkey became family. "Monkey kind of adopted me when I managed Bucky's," she explains. "Eventually I left the restaurant and bought the coffee shop across the road. I didn't feel bad about leaving Bucky's, but I sure felt bad about leaving Monkey. I knew my daily contact with him would end. By that time, Bucky's had basically been his home for seven or eight years. I took over the coffee shop on July first. Ten minutes after I opened that first day, there was Monkey. He'd never followed me anywhere before. Everyone on the island cared for him, but I guess I'm his soul mate!"

After a few months, Isabel remodeled the coffee shop, in the process creating a cubby for Monkey under her service counter, complete with built-ins for his bedding and bowls. She asked the contractor to install a cat door so Monkey could go in and out at night after closing. The man tried a standard cat door, but at seventeen-and-a-half pounds, Monkey was not your standard cat. The contractor switched it to a dog door.

"Monkey likes it back here in his kitty condo," Isabel reports, "but he's got his favorite places with the customers too. Like that chair over there–that's one of Monkey's spots. One day this customer came in and sat down on that chair. Well, Monkey just stood on the floor looking at him. Then his ears went back. I didn't want to make a big issue about it, but after the guy left, I made a little sign and taped it to the back of the chair: 'This chair is reserved for Monkey.'"

A friend of mine remembers seeing Monkey at the coffee shop one day. "He was sitting at a table with three women–his rump in a chair and his paws on the table, just like he was part of their meeting. Monkey was the only one without something to drink. I wish I'd had my camera!" Isabel confirms the story. "Sure, Monkey does that all the time."

"When I interviewed for this job," says Sorrel, a longtime employee, "Isabel said I had to like Monkey to work here. I thought she was talking about primates. It was a relief to

find out Monkey was a cat! When I come to work in the morning, there's always a long list of instructions: 'mix Monkey's specialty foods, fill bowl with half-and-half, crush vitamins, heat his bed-warmer.' In my next life, I want to come back as Monkey."

Isabel again: "Everybody on the island knows Monkey. He really is a people person. But sometimes it's like he says, 'If one more person touches me, I'm going to bite.' And he has, many times. Some people (men mostly) come up and just rumple him. They ask for it! Monkey attacks them. Claws and teeth. You can hardly get him to stop. But the people he goes after never complain. I guess they know they started it."

She fills in more of Monkey's history. "Monkey originally belonged to Frank D'Aquila who owned an Italian restaurant where Bucky's is now. Frank died unexpectedly when Monkey was about a year old. I remember Monkey wandered around a lot after Frank died. I worked at the grocery store then. Monkey came in, but people would shoo him out. Shop owners in the village looked after him and put out food, but the crows would get it. Monkey got a lot of love from people, but he had a hard life in a lot of ways, not having a family or a place to go at night. And of course, Bucky's closes in the winter. Monkey would sleep under the deck, and he had to scrounge for food and be on the lookout for dogs.

"Did you know he was snatched by an eagle once? People saw this huge eagle flying over the village with a cat in its talons. Someone yelled, 'Oh my God, it's Monkey!' He was throwing a fit, trying to claw and bite. The eagle carried him fifteen or twenty feet off the ground–way up there–then dropped him. Monkey disappeared under the deck at Bucky's for three days. When he came out, the vet treated him for puncture wounds.

"Almost everyone likes Monkey, but there are a few people who won't come into the coffee shop because he's here. A customer was kind of harassing him one day. I said, 'Leave Monkey alone.' The guy said, 'He's just a cat, he doesn't mind.' I told him, 'If you can't treat him gently, you'll have to leave.' You know what? The guy left. Of course, he came back later. It was pretty funny! Another time somebody made a remark about 'the dumb cat.' I said, 'You know, that cat is smarter than most of the people who come in here.' I didn't mean it, but I said it to the customer!" Isabel laughs. "You'd never think there was so much to say about one cat."

The next time I come in to hear more about Monkey, Isabel tells me he's been sick. "Jerry, his vet, tried a few things, but he wanted to get Monkey an X-ray. The vet's office here on the island doesn't have X-ray equipment so the choice was either take Monkey by ferry to a mainland vet or get him an X-ray at our human medical clinic. I chose the clinic." I ask Tytti, the clinic manager, about Monkey's X-ray. "Sure, we X-ray animals," she says. "Anything smaller than a horse. It's good customer service." I love this place.

Isabel explains that during Monkey's illness, the vet has been dropping in every day for a triple grande mocha and a check on Monkey. "Jerry gives Monkey shots almost daily. Despite all that painful poking and prodding, Monkey still loves him. When he hears Jerry's car pull up, he stands up, stretches, and ambles out to greet his friend. Of course, it doesn't hurt that Jerry always has a treat for him."

One morning I arrive at the coffee shop to tie up loose ends for the story. Monkey is nowhere around. There is a little handwritten sign on the counter: 'Don't ask.' Isabel clearly can't talk about it, but a customer tells me that Monkey is back at the vet's and he's very ill. The next days, full of hope and fear, are very hard for Isabel. Within a week, I get the bad news: Monkey has died.

A few days later, Isabel passes the word that there will be a wake at the coffee shop. She places an ad in our local newspaper inviting the community "to celebrate Monkey's extraordinary life." More than seventy-five people come, bearing food, songs, fresh flowers, Irish whiskey, stories, candles, photos, and one tin of imported sardines. Someone sets Monkey's chair on a table, an impromptu altar to hold the cards and memorabilia. Matt and Morgan play their fiddles. During the evening, I overhear a fellow admirer of Monkey's confiding to a friend: "You know, Monkey was the first person I met when I came to the island. I hope to God when I die, half this many people care about me!"

Cat Tale

Once there was a village cat.
He once was thin and then grew fat.

He wandered around from store to store
Where people fed him, then some more.

He sampled pastry, birds, and fish.
As years passed by, he made a wish.

His wish came true as time would tell.
He found his place with Isabel.

by Donna Beck

Shawn Westervelt and Cedar Chantey

Shawn, sixteen, and Cedar, fourteen, are brothers sharing an unconventional life—different fathers, different brothers and sisters from second and third families. They live together with their mom about half the year. Cedar lives the other six months with his dad across the island.

Lately they've been working on the kinks in their relationship, making an effort now that they're older to connect and draw together as brothers. "We've been flailing, but we're growing closer," says Shawn. "There's a lot we do now. We go out on Friday or Saturday night. We take in a movie or make some pottery, just little things. It's definitely made a difference."

We meet on this dark night in Shawn's eight-by-twelve-foot cabin, down a wet path from their mom's house. Tucked into thick woods, the place is cozy.

Cedar

With no electricity, candles are our light. A small propane stove heats the room. The cabin is filled with original artwork—framed, drawn on the walls, penciled, sketched, sculpted. Hand-lettered on the ceiling: Hear No Evil, See No Evil, Be No Evil.

The boys scheduled the interview around Cedar's homework. With finals coming up, he didn't want to meet when he had a heavy load. Cedar is a strong student. French, architecture, and power tech are his favorite classes. He sits relaxed tonight, the candlelight soft on his face. A quiet boy, he's not eager to jump in. "Nature has shaped me a lot. It changes me. I really love it. I love just going off into the woods." "Yeah," says Shawn, "the family calls him Eagle Eye. No matter where we go, he's the one who will find the giant agate, the best feather."

Both boys love guitar. Cedar plays in the band at school. Shawn just played his first club date, singing his own music at the Cookie Cafe on the mainland. They've invited him back in May. "Music is my passion, not only because I love playing, but because nothing else is a more true expression of emotion, longing, and love," says Shawn.

He goes on. "There are so many questions that I have. Who am I? Why am I here? Why am I so fortunate? Why are some not so fortunate? How should I best live my life? What am I supposed to learn from life? As I search for answers, I realize I may never know these things. But what I do know is that this world is a beautiful place. And this life is a beautiful thing, even though I don't understand any of it. I know that I'm glad to be alive. The biggest influence outside of my family is the search for love and the search for self. When I think about life, I think about myself as an undeveloped organism that's gonna take a lot more work. The more meditation I do, the more I'm getting into simplicity. I have a gnawing inside of me that wants to explore, that wants to grow."

Exploring is another interest the boys share. "I want to travel more, to know more worldly stuff," says Cedar. "I'd like the island to be a place to come back to. I want to experience more things, to see Rome, Greece, Egypt, France, Tibet, India—to see history for myself, not read about it in a book." He continues, his young face intense. "There are three main things that keep me going. One is every step up that I make in playing guitar. Second is listening to really good music. Third is sitting down when it's quiet and reading a really good book, like J.R.R. Tolkien's books. I want people to see me as a person. That I'm me."

"I'd like people to know how grateful I am for the strength that I have, for the people around me, and for the realization I have of how beautiful life is," says Shawn. "I was a really angry kid. Bullheaded. I don't know how my mom handled it. I've dealt with some of it now, awakened to not needing that anger any more."

It's been an hour. Time to blow out the candles, hike up the path, and get back to homework. Shawn pokes his head in the door of his mom's house before we drive Cedar back to his dad's. "Love you, Mom." He turns to Cedar. "Hey, Bro, you mind riding in the back?"

Darryl Davidson

The house is busy. In the adjoining living room, Darryl's three children, ages six to nine, have friends over. The four family dogs are the main attraction on this rainy, play-inside day. The whole place is frisky, dogs and kids. On the tube, the Bills are playing the Cowboys.

Darryl, thirty-three, sits at the kitchen table, calm as summer water. He's a big man with a deep dimple in his chin, an easy smile, and soft brown eyes.

Rhett, his youngest, zooms up to announce the score and ask his dad to peel him an orange. Darryl rolls the fruit between his hands for a moment, slips a thumb nail under the peel, and pulls the skin off piece by piece.

Handing it back to Rhett, he thanks him for the update. Smiling, Darryl turns back to us. "Now, where were we?"

Darryl grew up in the Snoqualmie Valley east of Seattle, where his family lived for five generations. He loved football and played varsity young, ranking All-State in his junior and senior years of high school. His hopes were high, and scouts were taking a look. Darryl's first month away at college, he tore up one knee. He blew the other one out in preseason play. "My career was over," Darryl says. So were his college years. "I only went to get a chance to play ball. It really was a hard time for me. Mom and Dad got a divorce that same year. It took me quite a long time to get focused again.

"You know, there was something else too. There was a car wreck the night of our homecoming game in my junior year. My best friend, Rhett Upton, and his brother Zack were both killed. Fell asleep at the wheel. It was a hard thing to get over…I don't know if I ever will, really. Our son is Rhett's namesake." Darryl is quiet now, in a faraway place. "I know I've lived my life differently because of Rhett's death. I have a lot of friends, but no one close outside of my family."

The early 1980s continued to be tough. "My dad and uncles owned a sawmill, and the timber business went belly up." Darryl moved home to his mom's, got a job in landscaping, made good money, had fast cars, "and racked up a lot of speeding tickets." There was some trouble on his twenty-first birthday: too much to drink with his buddies, a high-speed chase, and a car crash. "We thought we were invincible," he says. Miraculously, everyone walked away.

Once the trouble cleared up, Darryl's mom and grandpa sat him down, and urged him to go to Alaska. When the crabbing season opened, Darryl left on a catcher headed for the Bering Sea. "I loved it! I thought it was beautiful up there. But every time you go out, there's a good chance you're not coming back. At those temperatures, if you go overboard, you have just three seconds in the water. The problem is, well, a lot of things can happen. There's lots of money being made, but bad decisions happen. One time we were at St. Matthew, up there between Nome and Russia. We were eighty boats, counting the processors and catchers. A huge storm was coming. The skippers of twenty-two of those boats thought they could beat the weather and make the thirty-six-hour run back to Dutch Harbor." Darryl's boat was one of only eight that made it. The other fourteen went down in the storm.

Darryl explains how in an arctic storm like that, huge waves crash over the boat and ice the deck almost instantly. The vessel, now top heavy, can flip. So crews work around the clock: two men in survival suits and leather harnesses, chained on deck to keep from being swept into the sea, swing sledgehammers for two-hour shifts to crush the ice as it freezes on deck. "It always seemed like those storms hit at night."

67

You must not have time to think in a storm like that.

"No, you do! You really notice the color of the sea and the sky. Up there at St. Matthew, there are no trees. It's like you're real close to the sun and the moon. All that blue water, it's prettier than Hawaii."

Your boat was one of only eight that made it through the storm, and you talk about the beauty, not the terror?

"Well, I was ready to die. I mean, I loved my childhood, I wouldn't have changed it for anything. But coming from a logging community when the logging was over, the chips were always stacked against me. Forestry was my first love, even over football, and they had both been taken away. Having all that gone, well, I think it would almost have been a relief, you know, to end the struggle. At that time, I didn't really care."

After crabbing for two years, Darryl was ready for a change. He came to the island to visit his dad, who had remarried and started a tree service here. "Actually, he'd written me in Alaska and said I should come meet his children's new babysitter," Darryl says with a little smile.

Darryl and Lynn hit it off. They married in 1989 and moved to Seattle to find work. "We knew at the time we'd want to move back to the island to be near our families," he says. Five years later they made it happen, moving up and sharing a house with his dad. Darryl took a position at the grocery store. Recently he switched to the county road crew. "It's been really nice. I don't make a ton of money, but we've learned to live within a budget. I'd say I'm pretty successful. There's nothing that I don't have right now that I really want. So yes, I'd say I'm successful.

"I don't really try to put dreams out there any more. It's more day-to-day, but it feels fine. Rebuilding my dad's '67 truck is probably my biggest dream right now. You know, the one I haven't really talked about here is Dad. He's

probably my best friend." Darryl talks again about the tough financial circumstances his father experienced when the lumber business took its turn. "But you know, he did his best for us, and it was good enough. Now it's my turn. I definitely want to see my kids on to the start of their lives. Providing for them is what's most important to me now."

His daughter Dannyl comes up to the table with one of the pups. "Dad, Misty hasn't had her pill yet. I'm going to give it to her in this cheese, okay?" "Sure," he answers, "but that piece is a little big for her to swallow, maybe about half that size."

How about lucky breaks?

Darryl doesn't pause. "Lynn, she's the main one. I probably would have stayed in Alaska, and my number would have come up by now without her.

"What do I believe in? My family. That if you keep grinding away, you will make it. I don't ever want to see my kids go without. I was nine years old when I started working the sawmill. In high school we used to make five dollars a day. I've never had a vacation from work since I graduated high school. But my generation has turned the corner as far as having something to start with. By the time my kids are ready to go on, Lynn and I will be in a position to help.

"Each of my kids is different. Dannyl is really driven. She's gonna go and do big things, I think. I wouldn't say I'm a driven person; for me it's just survival. Michelle is the free spirit, the kind of person you wish you could be. And Rhett. I think I'll have to really be careful with Rhett. I don't want him to think he has to do something just because it was one of my loves in life. He'll have the opportunity to go a lot further than me. Each one of our kids has something I wish I had. It's fun to sit back and watch them. Each generation is getting a better chance in my family."

Chela Barnes

"You want me to talk about WHAT?"

Chela lets out a rowdy laugh. She's a graduating senior, a varsity player on the school's winning volleyball team, and an award-winning horseback rider. The philosophical questions we showed up with don't interest her much. Her days are spent on the court with her teammates, out in the barn with her horse, Gold, making college plans, or hanging out with friends.

Still, she'll give it a shot.

"I'm a happy person. Even when I'm sad, I can still laugh. I don't really know what keeps me going. I'm just basically happy.

"I think I carry a lot of emotion in me, but it's not ready to be expressed yet. I am letting more of it out, though, little by little. Some things are always there, but I blow them off. I just move on. I don't let things get really deep." Her voice drifts off. "I keep a lot inside. I guess I'm pretty private. Sometimes I can be really out there, though. My friend Amanda and I were talking the other night about what if we were in one of those

bave a girl. I mean, what if she grew up all frilly
and pink and afraid of horse poop?

plane crashes where everyone was killed. I wonder about those things sometimes but it's not a big part of my life.

"My best friend tells me, 'Walk on the wild side. Quit being so mature, so stable!' I guess that's just who I am. I see myself that way. I don't think I'm much different than a lot of people my age."

If you were to give advice to struggling young women, what would it be?

"I'd say do what makes you happy and you'll get through it. You just have to be strong. By strong, I don't mean be happy or joyous all the time. Sometimes being strong means not getting sucked into your problems, not dwelling on them. Sometimes it means having someone else believe in you."

Chela has experience there. At the end of last year, her mom made plans to move to Seattle. Determined not to change schools during her senior year, Chela looked for a way to stay on the island. Neighbors Stephanie and Tim Dies helped out. Steph and Chela had ridden horses together for years, and Chela had been babysitting the young couple's son, Jeremy, since he was born. "I'd been spending more and more time at their place. It wasn't like they formally asked me to move in or anything, it just kinda happened. At first Jeremy and I shared a room. Hey, that was interesting! Then Steph and Tim rented a bigger place so we could have more space. I don't know what I would have done without them. I don't want to think about it." Jeremy wanders up. She gives him a hug. "I wuv Chela!" he beams.

Will you want your own children some day?

"Yes, two! A boy and a girl, or two boys. I think I'd be afraid to have a girl. I mean, what if she grew up all frilly and pink and afraid of horse poop? It probably won't happen, but it could, anything can happen! When I'm a parent,

I'll probably give my kids more rules than I had. In my family, almost everything was up to me. In a way, I mainly made my own rules."

Posters, pictures, street signs, photos, and magazine pages cover her bedroom walls, floor to ceiling. There are newspaper clippings from winning volleyball seasons and a dozen ribbons and medals from her horse shows. A strip of yellow roadwork caution tape runs the border of the room. Out the window, Gold grazes the field.

"Through horses I learned a lot of responsibility. Financially I was responsible for most of my riding since about sixth grade. My mom would pay for a bag of grain or a lesson every once in a while, but I knew I had to work for most of it in order to buy my horse, get my saddle, and go to horse shows. Horses have also taught me about life. Working with them was a strong influence. It was a social thing too. I met tons of cool people, and got to adventure on my own. When I was sixteen, I went with a team to a competition in Utah for a week.

"I've had my problems, my ups and downs, but nothing major." Her junior year, Chela says, was pretty rough. Skipping class, "almost two months worth probably," she pulled some F's. This year things improved. She finished with a B average, the volleyball team took third at state, she rode a lot, and her studies were "pretty interesting." In the fall she'll go to community college. She's thinking of a career in veterinary medicine.

"There is something higher out there that has put us here. There's definitely a reason, or maybe many reasons, why we're here. I don't know if anyone has come up with the one answer, though, or if anyone ever will. There may be more than one answer. Hey, look at me." Chela lets loose that big, contagious laugh again. "My life is messed up, and I'm still happy. Figure that one out!"

71

Dorthalee Horne
Helen Lewis

Dorthalee and Helen, known on the island as Dort and Louie, walk out on their porch together. "Please, come on in!" Dort smiles, holding the screen door wide. Once everyone settles in, Louie offers Coca-Colas all around. She walks to the coffee table and picks up their photo album. "We've got quite a few pictures here," she says with a chuckle.

It's already a treat to be with these two.

Dort and Louie came to the island in 1945 looking for a break from busy careers in Seattle. Both were in physical education, Dort as a professor at the University of Washington and Louie teaching at Franklin High. "We knew we didn't want to teach all our lives. I'd always wanted a dude ranch," says Louie, "but we were interested in fish camps, too. It was during the war and there was gas rationing, so we saved our gas stamps and came up one weekend. We didn't even have a hundred dollars, but we had a dream."

They heard about acreage being released from a U.S. government landholding and came for a look. The forested property had no roads in, so their inspection was from the water side. The two fell in love with the beautiful little curve of the bay and the trees crowding down to the shore. With $3,000 borrowed from their families, they bought the sixty-three acres on Upright Head. But they had no experience in building. "We got a book," explains Dort. She goes to the shelf and pulls out a well-worn hardback, *How to Build Cabins, Lodges, Bungalows*, copyright 1940. "You bet we went to work!" Louie says. "We got a twelve-foot crosscut saw and a couple of axes and built ourselves a lean-to.

"We cleared the land and burned the brush. It took us two years coming up weekends and summers to build the first cottage. We hand-split the shakes from wood we gathered off the beach. My dad got us a keg of nails in Medford, Oregon, and shipped them up," says Louie. The women hired good help. "We pounded nails, but it was Bill Gallanger and Ross Spencer who were doing most of the construction by then. They said as long as they had their carpenter aprons on, they would charge us, but when they took them off, they wouldn't. Those two worked days and days for us without those aprons on!"

In the end, Dort and Louie built six rental units and named the place The Sea Ranch. Paging through the black and white snapshots, we see two young women in dungarees and work shirts smiling for the camera, their energy and joy captured on the page. "Here's one of Dort with a drink in one hand and a saw in the other!" says Louie proudly. Dort smiles, a little shy. "I never did learn how to use a power saw." They turn the pages together, looking back on their time.

There's a good story about their first summer here. "The word went around we were only here to get men. After that, no one would work for us without his wife coming along!" Louie lets loose another chuckle. Working so hard, they were also getting the reputation of being stuck-up. Dort picks up the story. "We decided to take some time off and go to an island dance, get to know folks a little. So we took the bar of Fels Naptha soap down to the bay, took our baths, got our dresses on, and went!" They didn't have much of a time. All the women were on one side of the room, the men on the other. Every third song or so, the crowd drifted out to their trucks for a drink. "Next time there was a dance, we wore

This year we got ourselves a nineteen-foot runabou

our jeans and shirts, brought our own bottle of Southern Comfort, and danced every dance. People accepted us then," Louie says, grinning.

"We had fun, but we worked awfully hard," Louie continues. "We were open all summer long, and in the winter for all the holidays and weekends. We did all the work ourselves, making the beds, chopping the wood, everything. In the end, we just got tired." Hearing them talk, it's hard to imagine how they shoehorned all this work in while keeping careers going in the city. "We never had a vacation," Dort adds. "We were always pushing." In 1963, after fourteen years, they sold The Sea Ranch. They retired from teaching nine years later and moved to the island full-time. "We thought if we could have just two good years of retirement…and what is it, twenty-five years now?" says Louie. "We've been so fortunate. I guess it's because we've led 'the clean life!'" Dort smiles.

Do you have advice for young people today?

Dort replies first. "Don't think there's anything you can't do. We both grew up with the idea if there's anything you really want, go about it with enthusiasm and energy."

"Today it seems kids live in the present," Louie answers. "I'd say, look to the future some, try to think about goals. At the same time, if you want to have your dream, start now. Don't wait until you have money. So often people lose their

dreams because they wait. Do things as soon as you can. Too many things in life change."

What has brought the most joy to your lives?

"Our partnership," says Dort, noting that they've been together close to sixty years now. "We've attained things together we could never have done alone. It's because we're so congenial …and because I give in to everything she says!" she laughs.

"We think of the other person first," Louie adds, serious now. "Dort is special. People just don't come along like her." Kindness fills the space between them; appreciation and respect walk hand-in-hand here.

We step out on the deck where their chairs are pulled up together. The manicured lawn slopes gently to the water with a glorious view of islands beyond. It's hard to believe these two are both over eighty. They seem decades younger. "This year we got ourselves a nineteen-foot runabout, a sexy little thing that just shoots around!" says Louie. "We like to go out to our special little haunts, oh, little bays around here, and have picnic supper and cocktails." Their poodle, Jigger, comes up, looking for a lap. "We might write a book ourselves one of these days. We sure have thought about it. There are just so many stories."

sexy little thing that just shoots around!

Tendercare

It's 9 p.m. on my hospice shift at Howard's house. Unexpected headlights turn up the driveway. A Jeep parks by the chicken yard, and our doctor, carrying his medical bag, walks up the wooden steps of the old farmhouse. He taps on the screen and, with our "come in," opens the door. "Hi, Howard. Just thought I'd drop in to see how you're doing." He kneels beside Howard's recliner. Putting his hand on the old man's thin shoulder, he asks again, "How are you tonight?" Howard talks about these visits for days after.

In our training, Gerri Haynes, a gifted hospice teacher, taught us to do just what Dr. Wilson did tonight. "Position yourself so your heart is on the same level as your patient's heart," she said. "People who are dying have had so many losses already. If you stand above them, you unconsciously take even more of their power. When you put your heart on the same physical level as theirs, you give them, give yourself and your relationship, strength. There's good reason for the old expression 'heart to heart.' It's about symbolic love and respect, and it works the same in any relationship. When your heart is on the same level with another person's, it's more likely to open up to them."

Position yourself so your heart is on the same level c

losses already. If you stanc

I don't think our doctor had to be taught this. I love watching him with Howard, the way he tunes directly into him, really hearing, really seeing him.

Dr. Wilson is still in his office clothes tonight, stone-washed blue jeans and a white cotton shirt. Even now, twelve hours after he began his day at the clinic, his vitality and warmth brighten the room. As he straightens and runs his hands through his short blond hair, he looks tired, though. Adjusting Howard's pain medication has proven tough. Too much makes him sleepy and causes hallucinations. Too little won't handle the pain. It's a delicate balancing act.

After visiting with Howard, he leaves new instructions for the caregiving team and heads home to his wife and two young daughters. As his headlights sweep past the fields of sleepy cows and turn onto the road, I switch the porch light off for the night. I've lived on the island for four years now, but this willingness of people to help each other still catches me unaware. Dr. Wilson is new here himself. Yet he came tonight, shaking off his weariness, stopping by to do what he could.

our patient's heart. People who are dying have had so many
bove them, you unconsciously take even more of their power.

When we asked Kristy and her daughter Bethy to do this interview, we hoped they would be able to speak about Diana. So we began, after a few minutes of small talk, by simply asking. Kristy nodded. Bethy spoke. "Diana lies very close to the heart."

Diana Johnstonbaugh died three and a half years ago on October 23, 1995. She was twelve years old. Her death came by suicide.

"We had a poster at the time of a forest waterfall tumbling over lush, green, mossy rocks," Kristy says softly. "It read: 'Without the rocks in its bed, the stream would have no song.' When Diana died, there was no water, no stream, no song. We had to find a way to put all the elements back together again. Find the water. Find the stream. Let the moss grow back."

After her sister's death "nothing was the same," says Bethy, who is herself thirteen now. "I didn't talk to anyone for about three months afterwards. I really didn't talk. When I went back to school, people pretended it didn't happen, pretended nothing was different. It was kind of weird because everything was different, but in a way it was easier to deal with than anything else they could have done."

"It was four or five months before I heard Bethy and her friends laughing. It took awhile for them to be able to come back together," Kristy says. "The best thing about living here is that everybody knows everything about everyone else …and the worst thing about living here is that everybody knows everything about everyone else. I could see it in people's eyes at the time. Sometimes I wasn't Bethy's mom …I wasn't even Diana's mom…I was just the mother of a suicide."

A tall glass of water sits untouched on the bench beside her. "Most people were very kind. It's amazing how many people know so much about suicide, how many have had some experience with it–their father, a sister, a friend, someone. A lot of people came and shared with me. It was like they were coming to say they could speak that language. When something that shattering happens…" Kristy pauses a long time, "your life…is…so…changed. You don't know how to express it. You have to teach yourself a new language, find a new way to communicate your emotions. And when other people come to you and use that language, connect and touch you with it, you don't feel so alone."

Tears slip down her cheeks. She reaches up and wipes them away. "It's as if the person I used to be died with Diana. I didn't know as much about people then. They all looked like they were whole. I thought I was the only one who was broken. Now I feel a lot softer toward people. I can feel more. I mean I tried to be that way before, but going through it in my own life I learned to be more compassionate. Once you experience something like that, you can become gentle. There's a strength in that gentleness that doesn't come until you've gone through it."

Kristy takes a deep breath and manages a smile. "Finding people to talk with about it is really a gift. I was planting flowers on Diana's grave one day, and this older woman came up to me. She put her hand on my shoulder. She said I was a 'local' now because I'd planted my heart here. 'Look around,' she said. 'Everyone has left their love here.' I think she was telling me that it wasn't just grief, sorrow, and death there, that, in a sense, the churchyard was a joyful place. I mean, it was so intimate the way she said it. 'Everybody's love is planted here.'"

She turns her eyes away for a few moments, then begins again. "Usually when people hear me talk about Diana, they hear me say how beautiful she was…she is…how intelligent and talented, how much I love her, how much I miss her. When someone dies, especially a young person, we tend to deify them. It can almost be like Romeo and Juliet. You know how people find their story so tragic but somehow romantic? I don't want anyone to think suicide is like that…romantic or in any way a good option. It's gritty. Raw. Ugly. It's *horrible*." Kristy stops. "These words aren't strong enough." She's crying softly now. "Suicide is soul-wrenching. It's *soul-breaking*. When Shakespeare wrote about Romeo and Juliet, he didn't finish the story. Their families and friends had to go *on*. I especially want young people to understand that.

"Hey, don't you guys want to talk about anything EASY, like what's my favorite color?!" She smiles a little. "Actually, it's easy for me to talk about these things. I really am okay

with this. I can talk about stuff from the heart because that's where I am, that's what I think about. It's small talk that's hard for me now. I just can't do it. I like to laugh too; it's kind of how I stay sane. I don't feel guilty about laughter. Diana loved laughing! Bethy does too. In a way, it's like our laughter honors her."

Bethy baked chocolate chip cookies today. She goes to the kitchen and brings them out to the deck. She is a quiet young woman, not venturing too much into this difficult conversation. But warmth shines past her shyness. Sitting in the morning sun, her golden hair streaming down her back, Bethy talks about her deep connection to plants, animals, birds, and the outdoors. She loves science and keeps a regular nature journal. "Being outside is important, not doing 'things,' just being," she says.

Do you have a favorite animal?

"All of them–except mosquitoes! Animals give me a lot of joy. I may want to be a biologist when I grow up." Her mom smiles. "Animals who are shy around everyone else go right up to Bethy. They love her, they sit in her lap. It's kinda cool to watch."

What do you hold dear, Bethy?

"My mom. She really has always been there for me. I can talk to her in a way I don't think any of my friends can talk to their parents." Her blue eyes light up. "And Shanny! I got him for my fifth birthday." "He's a generic yellow dog, a pound puppy," Kristy explains. "When she got him Bethy

said, 'Oh, hi, Shanny! That's what he says his name is!'"

Turning to Kristy: What do you hold dear?

"Bethy!" Leaning forward Kristy wraps both arms tightly around her daughter. "She's my blueberry-eyed muffin." They sit comfortably, hugging in the sun, no one speaking. Music floats outside, one violin playing a simple melody line from Bach.

With its back to a forest of evergreens, their cabin is a tiny, cozy A-frame situated high on a rocky promontory. The 180-degree view from their deck is of snowcapped mountains and islands dotting the emerald bay. "This place is a blessing for us. It is the gift of home," Kristy says.

We begin looking for a spot to take their photograph. Mother and daughter go barefoot, walking the dewy grass and warm rocks together. Bethy is first to see a chocolate lily flowering in the wild grass. A rare find. Shanny bounds up with a big rock in his mouth, nudging Bethy to play. After the photos, the two slip away together. We walk back toward the cabin with Kristy.

Do you feel joy these days?

"Actually, I do. That kind of amazes me. You let so much pain in, but along with that pain, everything is intensified, especially the happiness. I look at the color of the sky and sometimes it makes me cry with joy. I experience everything much more deeply.

"Sometimes the pain gets to be too much. I shut it off, but you know, after a few days or weeks I realize I'm not feeling anything. There's no pain, but there's also no joy.

When that happens, I remember to have a good cry. It isn't a hard thing to do; tears are always close to the surface for me.

"I think you have to work to keep your heart open. I actually use this image of opening cupboard doors. Inside my mind I reach in and open the doors one by one that I have shut off. If you can open to the pain and let it go, then the joy can be just as intense. Before something like this happens, you think, 'If I ever had to go through that, they'd have to lock me away in a padded room. I'd just go crazy.' I still can hardly believe I didn't. But look, it's three years later and here we *are.*"

Kristy takes a long breath. "I think what's meant to happen is what happens…even with Diana." She pauses.

When she begins again, her words come very slowly. "I don't know why Diana died. I'm not claiming to know why. I just need to trust that maybe she needed to learn something from it…or I needed to learn something from it…or the other people who have been touched by her. I mean, her death affected everybody so deeply. All we can do is try to learn from it. I'm sure it's about learning a better way to love."

Walking up the path to leave, something catches my eye. It's Bethy, perched very high in the branches of a huge old madrona tree. Blending into the green leaves and red bark as naturally as a wood nymph, she sits relaxed and still, looking silently out over the water.

*I was planting flowers on
Diana's grave one day, and
this older woman came up to
me … She said I was a 'local'
now because I'd planted my
heart here.*

Gary Franco

The moon was still out at 5 a.m. when Gary arrived at his fields to cut nine bunches of tulips and fifteen bunches of daffodils. He sent them off FedEx to Connecticut at 9 o'clock. His mom won't be surprised. These bundles of Northwest springtime arrive every year on her birthday, enough for bouquets in every room.

We meet later, when the sun is warming the day. Gary has one of those faces—when he smiles, his whole face breaks into joy. The eyes give it all away; there's a kid at play inside this forty-five-year-old.

We walk the fields, talking about the years he and his wife Alberta spent building Madrona Farms. They moved here in 1974

Franco

"as rebellious hippies." By 1976 they had begun their business. "This was a happening place, the fields filled with flowers and berries. It was intense, hard, inspiring work. I loved it! I'd listen to Van Morrison as I drove in with my cup of hot coffee each morning. My great crew was out there picking, people were buying, it was exhilarating!" Some of their produce was sold in the islands, but most sold at their farm stand in Seattle's Pike Place Market, open seven days a week, ten months a year. Eventually the intensity of commuting as "a freeway warrior" and the hours spent managing the business got to be too much. "There was no time to put my fingers in the dirt. It took the inspiration out of it," he says. Since 1995 Gary and Alberta have simplified the operation, growing only daffodils, tulips, and berries for their jam business.

"Right now I'm kinda hanging out with my boy Lucas and his friends. I really enjoy being around children these days. I haven't given up on adults, mind you; it's just that children have such promise.

"Something that really shook me to my rafters was the suicide we had here a few years ago. That's when it hit me. How could that happen? She just slipped through all of our fingers. I want to make sure that doesn't happen again. Kids need a group, an activity, an individual to turn to. It was a real wake-up call to me. What about my kid? He's just twelve. Did I know his friends? Did they know me? I knew I wanted to get more involved in our community. That's where I'm getting most of my inspiration these days, being around kids. Sports is my way, but it's just one vehicle. There are other ways of reaching kids too, like music and the arts. I enjoy working with the local kids. I haven't met a kid on this island I don't like.

"I have a great deal of admiration for the job being done in our schools, but even with teachers and parents working as hard as they are, it's just not enough. I think there needs to be more energy focused on children. Kids need more support. I think we've been neglectful, too distracted by television and materialism. We've gotten out of focus. I believe our priorities are mixed up. We put too much energy in the wrong places, not enough where it counts. Like acquiring junk. What do we do with it? We sure can't take it with us.

"I think children need—it's hard to find the right word here—I think it's good for them to have something beautiful, a belief in something or someone more wise and more powerful than we humans. Having religion can be a comforting thing for all of us. I'm more into religion now than I've ever been. I was raised Catholic, but here I go to the community church. Have you heard of Jesse Winchester? He's an American folk singer from Biloxi, Mississippi. He's got this song 'You Can't Stand Up All By Yourself.' He sings about the need we have for the touch of a mighty hand. Call it God, whatever, a mighty hand. That song is humbling, good for me."

83

Gary Franco

As he talks, Gary absentmindedly picks a few dandelions, gesturing with the little bouquet as he continues. "But look, I've only been in this community twenty-three years. There are lots of folks who've been around twice as long as me, who've done twice as much. You're wasting your time talking to me. I'm just an upstart here."

This scenario is becoming familiar, people saying their story isn't rich enough to write about. On this island, people are eager to point to others whose stories need to be told. We remind him if we could, we'd interview everyone here. The process is about learning what people feel, what brings meaning to their lives.

With that, Gary heads straight back where he started, family. "Mom is Irish, hot-blooded. Dad was Italian. My father had sixteen kids. He taught me if you're dishonest in your dealings it will come back and get you, keep you awake at night. He worked too much and stressed too much. He was rough, violent in ways. Rather than judge my dad, I

have to just say he did the best he could with what he had.

"I like getting older. I like my hair turning gray. The older I am, the less I care what other people think. I am who I am. If I have a certain belief and someone disagrees, tough." He stops, looking uncomfortable. "That's not really what I meant to say. I do care what people think." He pauses for a minute, trying to match up both ends of his belief. "It's just that I'm not going to try to be something I'm not, in order to please. Let's not take it so seriously. It's okay to disagree."

Walking back though his fields, still holding the little bouquet, Gary adds a final comment. "You know, I have thought about the meaning of life. The best thing I've come up with relates to these plants right here. It's our job as adults is to provide fertile soil for the next crop coming up. We can try to follow the Golden Rule. We can be good examples."

. . . look, I've only been in this community twenty-three years. There are lots of folks who've been around twice as long as me, who've done twice as much. You're wasting your time talking to me. I'm just an upstart here.

Kelly, fifteen, sits on her deck munching a cookie. In blue cutoffs and a tank top, she wears no earrings, no fingernail polish, no jewelry, no makeup. She is simply Kelly.

Listening carefully to the questions we offer, she takes time answering. "I need a lot of support. I'm dependent on people on an emotional level. Like with my friends, I can tell them everything. I am very emotional. I need people to tell me it's okay to be emotional. If I'm around people I know and trust, then I feel protected.

"I'm shy, very much an introvert. People scare me, especially off the island. You hear about kidnappers and that you can't trust anyone. It's a message that's going around. It's really depressing." Her dark brown eyes are intense. "I like to trust people. Trusting people puts me at ease.

"The hardest part of my life so far," she says softly, "was when my friend Diana died." Kelly is quiet. She sits still. She looks at her hands in her

She

lap. Tears slide down her cheeks. She wipes them away, but they just keep coming. She lets them come. This is so hard. There is nothing to say, no way to take away this sadness. Diana's suicide, at age twelve, is a question without an answer.

"I don't think I'm quite old enough to know about life yet," Kelly says finally. "It's one of those things on the horizon for me." She pauses, then continues. "But I don't think we're just here by some miraculous chemical mixture. I don't really like to question why we're here. I just like to *be* here, I like to live. Mostly it's important to accept things, I guess. If you can't change something, don't try. Focus on what's important in life."

For this young woman, that means friends, family, and her pets. "Animals and family are important to me—my dog Brady, my cat Kitty, my horse Dezzy. Working outside with my horse relaxes me. The sounds, the air, everything about being outside is good.

"The best part of my life is having my mom. I love my mom. She is always there for me. She is very supportive. I can totally count on her. All my friends love her. She's fun, very fun. She's the funnest mom I know! For me, life would be very hard without her."

Another important piece of Kelly's life is Spring Street School, a small, private school on the next island. About twenty local kids ride the ferry over and back each day to attend. The student body there totals about sixty students, sixth through twelfth grade. "It's like family," Kelly says. "I love it! The teachers really care about us. The kids support each other. With the kids' attitudes and the teachers' caring, it makes it easier to be smart at Spring Street. I took on a lot of challenges when I started. I was behind in some areas and

had to work hard." She won honors for the most improved student in ninth grade and says she's looking forward to tenth. "This year our class took a trip to Belize, Guatemala, and Mexico. Going to the ruins of Tikal in Guatemala was nifty. On the trip we camped a lot, and slept out in hammocks. We went to these small villages. It was a life-changing experience."

She stays connected with her friends here through volleyball, playing varsity on the island team. "Last year one of our most fun games was one we lost! It's always fun to be faced with a challenge, to try to overcome it. For me sports are good either way, win or lose, but I'm not that way with board games. I like to win those! Last night my mom, some friends, and I played Monopoly. I cleaned house!"

Kelly likes exotic clothes, bold clothes, clothes with drama, clothes that make a statement. "They help me have fun. I love to go searching for special things. I got my velvet pants in Fan Tan Alley in Victoria. I can't stand pink clothes, though. Ugh! Pink is the most awful color ever invented!"

Her room is a menagerie of stuffed animals, maybe seventy-five fuzzy friends sitting on the bed, the bookcase, all around. One teddy bear in the corner wears Kelly's sunglasses perched on its nose. Another swings over her bed, dangling a pair of long, black evening gloves. A string of twinkly, white Christmas lights outlines her closet doors. A little herd of plastic ponies prances on one shelf, a Lego castle guards another. What about this side of you, Kelly? "I like to laugh, especially at myself. It helps a lot when people laugh. I can't handle it when people can't laugh. It's like my favorite quote from *Willy Wonka*: 'A little nonsense now and then is relished by the wisest men.'"

Summer Moon Scriver
and Jaime Cordova

We take a narrow path from the dirt road. Walking through knee-high brush, we come to a little clearing in the trees with a shed, a few chickens scratching around in the salal bushes, and a sixteen-foot trailer. A dog charges out, barking wildly.

Inside the little trailer is a different world. A baby has come.

Father and mother, young and new themselves, are vibrant with the importance of this moment. Life is happening. Reality is in focus. Their son is a few weeks old, but it feels as if birth is still going on. Birth of awareness. Birth of joy.

The infant, in his father's arms, is alert and calm. "When I cut his cord, I said, 'Okay, this is it. You have your own independent life now.' I want to fill his life with music, art, and abundance but, in the end, it's whatever he wants. We're just here to guide him."

A song plays ever so softly, "The love you make is equal to the love you take." The Beatles' gentle harmony feels made for this new family. It is one of those rare moments

when time itself seems to breathe deep, becoming slow, nourishing, simple.

The baby's birth came on the night of the lunar eclipse. "Right after the shadow of the earth passed over the moon my labor happened," says Summer. "Cosmos was born at 1:45 a.m. I could feel every tree, every plant. It was different. *Different*, as if the whole *land* was being born. I have been in awe since he has come. The days are passing. I spend time just looking at him, talking to him, thinking of our life together, thinking of the experiences I want to share with him. We have a little stream on our land. I want to take him down there, to listen."

He was born in this cozy room overflowing with necessity. Dishtowels and pots and pans dry by the sink. A clutter of dishes, cups, and utensils sit on open shelves. Beside the wood stove: a chopping block, a hatchet, and a cardboard box of kindling. Overhead, five cast-iron frying pans hang along a log beam. Arranged largest to smallest, they give a feeling of order, of art, to the little room. A ribbon of scarlet chili peppers dances the length of the beam. A potted primrose blooms on the windowsill.

89

Jaime puts the baby in Summer's arms. She settles into the sheepskin on the rocker. The creaking rhythm of the chair is a chant, a heartbeat. The baby snuggles in close, finding her breast.

What prepared you for this baby?

"Our love," says Jaime. "And this land. The baby brought this land to us definitely. If you look back how it happened, we conceived in late June and bought the land in August. When we bought it, we didn't know Summer was pregnant."

"I felt I was definitely ready when I found out," Summer says. "It felt really good. This baby was made with a lot of love. He has a strong community on the island. The whole pregnancy I didn't have any fears. I felt the community was here for us so strongly."

"We call him Cosmos, but he doesn't have his official name yet," Jaime continues. "In the Tlingit tradition, you give a child a nickname when he is born. When he becomes eleven or twelve, he will choose his own name. This little one has five grandparents and three great-grandmothers. It was really special to have all the grandmas here for the birth. They came for the whole month."

Could you talk more about life, where you find its joy and meaning?

Summer smiles. "For me it's definitely living off the land. And our hopes for Cosmos. I think he'll have a great life! What better than to be born on your own land, under your own cedar trees? We look forward to watching this place change. Listening to the birds. Having a piece of it. This little guy here will have land and security that way. It's pretty magical to be the caretaker to a beautiful piece of earth, to try to treat it well as it is treating us well."

Jaime answers now. "This miracle of life, that's what keeps me going. I really love living in the present, but with my eyes on the future. I look at the past to reflect and learn from it." He is eager to talk, to put words around his feelings. "My country is the earth. Meaning comes for me in the sun rising every morning. In the deer. This land. The eagles. The wildness. In our hearts beating. Also I find it in what I see in my family's life, the several communities we are a part of, not just here, but in Mexico. We gather. We humble ourselves to the earth, to the Creator, and give thanks."

In the Tlingit tradition, you give a child a nickname when he is born. When he becomes eleven or twelve, he will choose his own name.

Doing "The Dump"

When visitors come, there's the "must-do" list: kayak one of the picture-postcard bays, hike a beach at low tide, rent bicycles for the day, get a treat at Holly's world-class bakery…and go to The Dump.

Also known affectionately as "The Mall," "Take It or Leave It," and "Neil's Nordstrom," The Dump is a landmark, a gathering place, a hangout, a locale of community pride. For me, it holds the heartbeat of our community, in some ways representing the best in our little universe.

Living on an island provokes the practical and ecological question of what to do with leftover stuff. The dumpsters are here for true trash, but what about the decent castoffs, things we've replaced or upgraded? And then there are the items one step down the food chain—the jacket with the broken zipper, the cracked $40 designer vase that still holds water, the Bart Simpson mouse pad—all serviceable, but tilting toward tacky. Out here there's no truck that rolls up collecting for Goodwill. We take it to The Dump.

To clear up any confusion, "The Dump" doesn't refer to the trash collection area, the recycling center, or the trailer-size dumpsters in our county Transfer Station. It's the part of that property that houses our ongoing version of a community garage sale every Wednesday, Saturday, and Sunday, noon to 4:00. Except at this garage sale, there's no sale. "Shoppers" here find everything–computers, jeans, power tools, doll beds, canning jars, electronic components, pogo sticks, shoes, elk antlers, leather furniture, and one of the best collections of preowned magazines in the entire Northwest, all for free.

A sign reading, "You Have Two Choices: Take It or Leave It" hangs up high on the green shed-style metal building that houses the operation. A wooden table, shaded by an old canvas umbrella, squats up front. The tabletop is a jumble of the day's dropoffs. An alder tree leans in close, its leafy branches stretching right inside, where toaster ovens, televisions, hair dryers, computers, and vacuum cleaners are arranged neatly in the appliance/electronics section. People beehive in and out, browsing, swapping news, visiting, catching up, and playing the odds they'll be there when "the good stuff" gets dropped off.

My friend Peggy and her teenage daughters live in the city where shopping at Nordstrom, Eddie Bauer, and mega-malls is a regular event. But when they're here, they say Neil's is the mall they never miss. Whether they are browsing the cubbies of neatly folded clothing, checking out a box of old McCall's dress patterns, discovering a stash of Christmas lights, finding a vintage John Lennon CD, or spending lazy time paging through back copies of *Utne Reader, Chemical & Engineering News, Martha Stewart, Organic Gardening, Forbes, National Geographic,* or any of seventy titles on the rack, this is where they want to be on Sunday afternoon.

Over the years I've gotten good stuff here. My oldest son furnished his first apartment from The Dump, including his couch, chairs, and TV. My favorite find was an oversized wooden picture frame with words hand-stenciled around the border: "Remember, there are no bad people, just tight shoes."

A fifth-grader from a well-to-do island family informed me once that she did all her clothes shopping here. "Every-thing except underwear and shoes," she said, obviously proud of the reverse elitism. "You can find *everything* there. Sometimes I only take home brand names, other times I don't care. Every once in a while I get funky things that I wear a few weeks, then I take them back and look for something else."

Clearly there's a connection to the national teenage trend of bargain hunting at Value Village, Goodwill, and Salvation Army, but something else is at play here too. Tourists come, locals come, people of all ages and backgrounds come to soak up the atmosphere of the place. What is it?

"I think it has to do with the 'gift economy' that functions here," explains Ona Blue, who single-handedly organizes the mountain of incoming merchandise in her twenty volunteer hours behind-the-scenes each week. "The world we usually live in is an exchange economy. Here at The Dump we're a gift economy. I think it represents being able to have what you want. That does something important for the child in each of us.

"I believe in people getting their needs met," she continues. "I feel like if everyone got their needs met in this world, there wouldn't be greed. That's why I can spend my time going through the boxes, the piles of things coming in. This fills that part of me that needs to do something helpful, something beyond myself."

Neil Hanson, site manager of the Transfer Station, including the section that locals playfully give his name, picks up the theme. "It's extremely counter to our cultural conditioning, this gift economy concept. It is a valuable experiment. I think it could be done in other places. There doesn't seem to be any stigma about shopping here. People of all income levels come. I heard one person give a good analogy about it. Referring to the Reagan-era policy of trickle-down economics, this person said that here at Take It

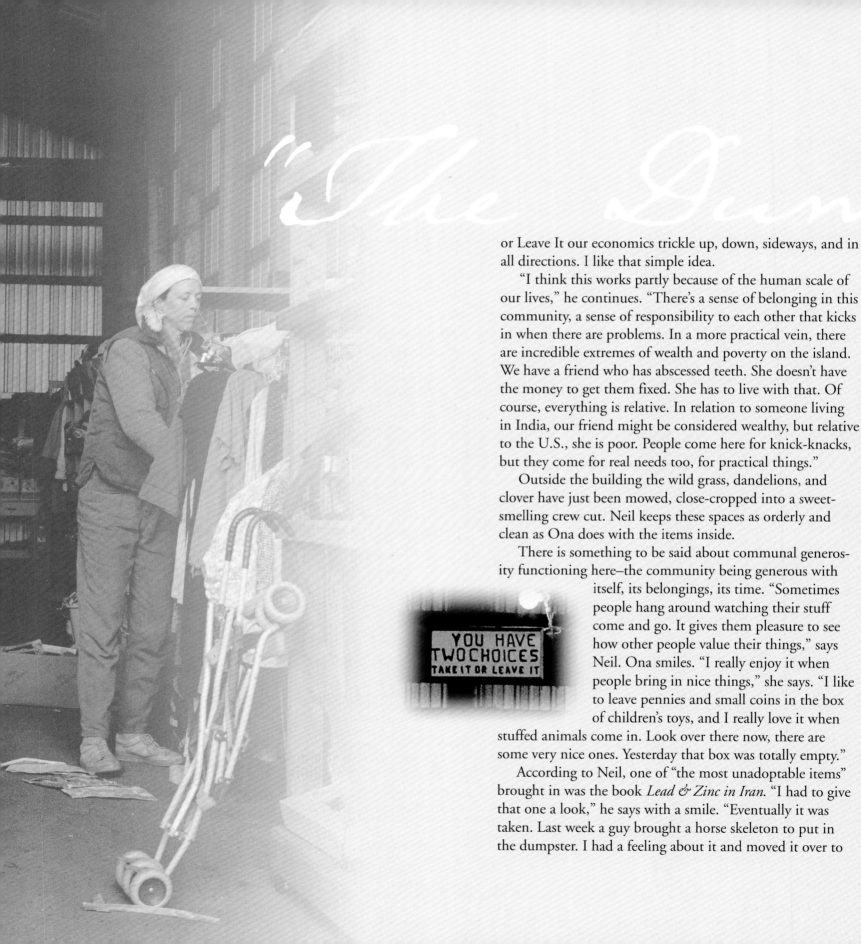

or Leave It our economics trickle up, down, sideways, and in all directions. I like that simple idea.

"I think this works partly because of the human scale of our lives," he continues. "There's a sense of belonging in this community, a sense of responsibility to each other that kicks in when there are problems. In a more practical vein, there are incredible extremes of wealth and poverty on the island. We have a friend who has abscessed teeth. She doesn't have the money to get them fixed. She has to live with that. Of course, everything is relative. In relation to someone living in India, our friend might be considered wealthy, but relative to the U.S., she is poor. People come here for knick-knacks, but they come for real needs too, for practical things."

Outside the building the wild grass, dandelions, and clover have just been mowed, close-cropped into a sweet-smelling crew cut. Neil keeps these spaces as orderly and clean as Ona does with the items inside.

There is something to be said about communal generosity functioning here–the community being generous with itself, its belongings, its time. "Sometimes people hang around watching their stuff come and go. It gives them pleasure to see how other people value their things," says Neil. Ona smiles. "I really enjoy it when people bring in nice things," she says. "I like to leave pennies and small coins in the box of children's toys, and I really love it when stuffed animals come in. Look over there now, there are some very nice ones. Yesterday that box was totally empty."

According to Neil, one of "the most unadoptable items" brought in was the book *Lead & Zinc in Iran.* "I had to give that one a look," he says with a smile. "Eventually it was taken. Last week a guy brought a horse skeleton to put in the dumpster. I had a feeling about it and moved it over to

Take It or Leave It. There was a lot of interest from the tourists. By the end of my shift, every bone was gone, all taken bit by bit." Occasionally things will be dropped off that the two don't think are appropriate: a box of ammo once, certain magazines, violence-based toys. Those they throw out. "This place is definitely for the whole family," Neil says.

Sometimes, looking at our own history, we see footprints in our childhood, hints of the person we will later become. "We both remember reading the book *The Boxcar Children* when we were little," says Ona. "It's a novel about kids who went to the dump for all their needs. I think I read it five times." Neil adds, "It was an enchanting book for both of us. It apparently had an impact."

There is an air of sweet innocence around Neil and Ona, but it marries resoluteness, a solid vein of ore. Their long hair, casual clothing, and light spirits mirror the feeling of the 1960s. So does their commitment to what they value. Together for almost fifteen years, they live in a handsome, hand-built bungalow in one of the island's two affordable housing communities. Choosing not to own a car, they bicycle or walk here on the island and use regional transit on the mainland.

"I've had a significant number of people suggest this become an actual store," says Neil. "Both Ona and I are totally committed to that never happening. Never. As it is, this place is something completely outside of most people's experience, and in that way I feel it is valuable."

Julie van Camp

The wooden sign reads Van Camp. We turn off the main road onto a leafy lane. Two tire tracks, with a thatch of grass between, lead off into the distance. Overhead, branches of alder, mountain ash, and maple arch together. Sunlight slips through the canopy and sprinkles the ground with summer freckles.

Finally, the trees thin out and the view opens wide. To one side a guest cabin tucks into a stand of firs. To the right sits a sturdy swing set, a sand pile, and a child-sized wheelbarrow full of plastic garden tools. The centerpiece is a large Northwest-style home.

Classical music is playing as Julie welcomes us inside. The place is lovely–paintings on the walls, oriental rugs on the hardwood, a stone fireplace. Large windows showcase the view of lawn and garden, with water and islands beyond. Julie offers steaming cups of tea. "Let's talk outside, on the trails or at the beach!" she says. "I could *live* outside."

We walk the property, choosing a narrow trail along a high bluff overlooking the water. Julie's corgi pups, Gabby and Karma, romp ahead. At a driftwood bench on a dramatic lookout, we stop. Our conversation begins with Julie talking about family, but mid-sentence, she swivels and points a finger out over the waves. "Can you tell me what kind of bird that is?" We watch it silently soar and scout the water.

She turns back with a smile. "You ask what thrills my heart? It's grandchildren! Nine years ago our daughter Lisa had twin girls, born more than three months premature. Ashley weighed just over one pound; Lindsey, two pounds. Ashley was so tiny even an incubator was too big. They put her in a little box with cellophane over the top. Her skin was so thin it felt like you could almost see through her. But she had ten tiny fingernails and ten toenails. That's when I knew there were miracles."

Our conversation ranges wide and rich. The joy Julie takes in studying her Iowa roots pops into a discussion of her work in the court system. A quote from the Persian mystic Rumi shows up in a story she tells about her pups.

"I don't know what's in me that I have to get to the top of the mountain or the end of the trail," she says. "Mountain climbing was my present to myself when I turned fifty." She enrolled in Lou Whitaker's week-long mountain school and climbed Mount Rainier. "Actually, when we made our climb, the snow was wet and yucky. We got to the top and couldn't see a thing." That was just for starters.

Next Julie signed on with a group headed for Nepal and the Himalayas. They were gone thirty-six days. Her story includes mythical names: Katmandu, Everest, Kala Patar. "We trekked to Sagarmatha. That's the Buddhist name, the real name, of Everest. I believe it means Mother Goddess of the Earth. We made base camp at 17,500 feet. We couldn't go farther without spending huge amounts for climbing permits. We went on to the highest non-expedition peak in Nepal, Mount Mera, at 22,000 feet." She tells of climbing over the Cholai Pass carrying a thirty-five-pound pack. The hand-over-hand climbing was too steep for the yaks that had carried their gear.

"In our group I was the tortoise, not the hare. I didn't want to rush to our next camp and then hang around talking. I wanted to know what it was like along the way. You wake up to recognize that the present is where life *really* is. You can't be present with yourself if you're always looking ahead to where you want to be. Too often we focus on the distance and miss the bird right here on our path."

After the Everest trip, Julie's husband, Rip, took up climbing too. She laughs, quoting him: "'What do you mean,' he said, 'you're not going to leave me *behind*?'" There's tenderness as she continues. "Rip gives me freedom and structure too. He gives me a safety net and never says 'no, you can't do this.'"

She tells about visiting Thyangboche Monastery in Nepal. "You feel a sense of grace and awe in a place like that. Their music must be one of the deepest sounds there is. Those long horns! They bellow. They resonate. I guess they're calling their spirits. Being there had something to do with being present to the experience without having to totally understand it. It was about going inside, but not just into your heart. That music goes from the tip of your toes to the top of your head. You feel nourished hearing it. It's not like food that we eat and it is gone. It's with you forever. You just have to call it up. It's certainly strength and armor against some of the cloudier times."

Being out in the elements is where Julie is in her own element. Later we sit on the porch of her guest cabin. It's cozy, simple, quiet here. This is the piece of life she lets herself treasure more and more, her transition out of main-stream business into personal business.

"In your sixties, it's very important to have a project as your professional life is, by choice, waning. Mine is geneal-ogy. It's a passion for me! My heart is in the black dirt of Iowa. My father was a pediatrician, so we lived in town, but

though I wasn't raised on the homestead farm, my roots are there. All my relatives were farmers, eight generations! These people that lived two centuries ago are *alive* for me today.

"There is a spiritual side of me that I have room for now. Each morning I begin by going to my office for twenty minutes of spiritual reading, then I take the dogs for a walk. I try to live by three suggestions I found in one of my morning readings: develop a stronger faith, live a simpler life, and give a helping hand. This time in my life is a privilege. I feel so grateful. I think it's the greatest stage. I'm learning to round off the rough edges.

"The beauty is having *time* at this stage. And balance. It's such a basic, simple, everyday word, 'balance.' It's like the water out there, the troughs and the highs. Life would be dull, having only the highs. I first read *The Prophet* when I was fourteen or fifteen. Do you remember how Gibran talks about the shallow water, how it pounds the shore, kicks up, makes lots of noise? But when you get into the deep water …now that's where your soul is.

"I lost three very close friends, all from breast cancer. But I haven't really lost them. I mean, I can't pick up the phone and just *call*, but they're still part of me. You carry the thoughts, emotions, and feelings of love with you when someone dies.

"God is here in everything, outside, inside, around all of us. I don't think the Buddhists or the Sikhs are wrong. We all come from the heart of God. I think we can find the wisdom of God in each other, in everyday people every-where. It's all a matter of love, the overwhelming presence of God in all we see."

You wake up to recognize that the present is where life really is.

o often we focus on the distance and miss the bird right here on our path.

Babylon Jasmine Koruv

Andy Murphy, twenty-one, goes by the name Babylon. "Originally I just liked the sound of it, 'Babylon.' But sometimes I tell a different story—that I've taken the name as a way to steal power from material society. Babylon represents the greatness of the material world, and the material world robs meaning from people's emotions and morals. It overshadows the spiritual world. By stealing its name, I want to steal its power."

He rents a room in an old two-story house he shares with friends. When we arrive, he's downstairs on the couch reading a library book. It's the latest of five he's read in a few weeks. He likes science fiction, fantasy, and "nonfiction that deals with the powers that rule the world."

His last two years since high school graduation have been full. Babylon spent a year or so studying social science and computers at The Evergreen State College in Olympia. After starting out in campus housing, he moved to a treehouse in the woods. "It was free. Besides, I liked my roommates better in the treehouse. People would come and go. We had up to six at a time there. We didn't have electricity or running water. Basically we were squatting." Babylon likes the term "squatting" better than "living on the streets." "Well, we weren't actually on the street, you know. But, then again, being where we were was basically illegal. I mean we weren't *supposed* to be there."

It was about this time he met Nava. They became engaged and got an apartment together. Eventually they left school and headed for Hawaii, but the islands weren't what they expected. "There were no jobs, not even at McDonald's. I used my student loan money for living expenses." They moved to Anchorage, Alaska, near Nava's mom. "It was very beautiful up there, nice parks too, but the city is full of violent, racist people who could be really ugly." They decided to return to Olympia.

Babylon came back first. He stayed in an abandoned railroad tunnel while trying to find housing. He discovered the place when a street friend who lived there asked him to

take care of his dog one night while he was away. "The railroad tunnel wasn't all that different from the treehouse. There was more room, plus I didn't have to deal with people being upset that I was on their property. There were already some mattresses there. I had my own sleeping bag. Squatters aren't dangerous. They don't have any place else to go, so they have to keep themselves under control. And it's a matter of respect. When you don't have anything, you look out for other people who don't have anything."

Nava moved back, but things didn't work out. "We broke up and there were a whole lot of troubles. Lots of stuff happened." One day he sent his mom an e-mail saying goodbye. "Then I tried to kill myself." His mother called the police. They arrived, talked things over, and suggested Babylon get a psychiatric evaluation. That led to his decision to check into a mental hospital. He stayed five days.

"It wasn't scary there. Really it was pretty quiet. I'd been hanging out with crazy people already; just up till then, it was in an unsupervised environment." His words come out in tight, staccato bursts with long, thoughtful spaces in between. "My main impression was the place was really, really boring. I could sit around and read old magazines, basically have therapy a couple times a day, eat, and sleep. We could wear those hospital pj's if we wanted to. I did. The place was painted pale green. I think the color was supposed to help lower the

It's a classic outback oilskin. It's got really big pockets. That help cards, my toothbrush, and contact lens case…Everything I need

tension, but it made things boring. But boring was what I needed. After the railroad tunnel, the house I'd been living in had been trashed; everyone around me was either suicidal or homicidal. One roommate had multiple personalities. The most well-adjusted person there had scars up and down her arms from razors. There was a suicidal junkie guy who saw angels."

Why did you try suicide?

"For one thing, I was hanging around with a lot of people who were suicidal. And it was partly about the breakup with my fiancee. Everything was falling apart." Babylon found a group on the Internet who planned suicide. He'd go on line and check in with them. "I believe in reincarnation, so I really wasn't choosing to leave as much as I was choosing to start over. I think escaping life is a lot more difficult than just taking yourself out. I haven't even come close to being actively suicidal since I came out of the hospital.

"Right now I'm just kind of surviving, figuring out where I'm going next. I'm looking forward to going to Seattle to be part of the World Trade Organization protest later this month. That's important to me. It makes me feel like I'm making a difference. It's a big ambition, trying to shut that meeting down."

We ask about his clothing style. "I go through periods. For a while I wore a tie and looked really straight." A long, black Australian-style coat is his current trademark. "My mom bought it for me. It's a classic outback oilskin. It's got really big pockets. That helps a lot with tarot cards, my toothbrush, and contact lens case. I carry a few letters from my friends. Everything I need is in my pockets."

Can you talk about your beliefs?

"If I had a magic wand, I'd make it so everyone was fed and no one had more than two kids. I don't have rules really.

The main things I worry about are community and class struggle. I think a sense of community is really lacking in the U.S. That's one of the things I like about living on the island. I try to do what I can to keep things going, getting together with people, staying connected. I like hanging out with my friends, going out for a walk, or taking a hike. I keep trying to get someone to go fishing with me. Part of being in a community like ours is knowing you'll see people you really can't stand and being nice to them anyways. I'm not being sarcastic. I have to be nice to them, but they have to be nice to me too, and they are.

"A lot of my world view is Buddhist, and there's a part you could call 'Island Pagan,' which has elements of Celtic and Native American traditions. For me that's about respect for nature, having a sense of community, and the sacredness of the four directions.

"The role of love in my life is that it almost got me killed. I think it's very, very dangerous. Of course, there are different kinds of love. There's the friendly kind I feel in this community that helps keep me alive, helps keep me happy. On the other hand, there's romantic love. You can really lose yourself there, especially if you lose the person you've in love with, then boom—there's nothing left. Family love is a friendly love, a very healthy thing. I get along really well with my sister. She's probably the only one who understands me on a really deep level.

"I like computer work and Web page design. I do piece-work too, like dishwashing. My main ambition is music right now. I play the drums, sing, play a little keyboard. What I'm really hoping is I'll be making my living traveling, playing gigs. My music is rock and roll with a lot of punk and a little reggae influence."

We ask if he'd sit at his drums for a photo. "Sure." Babylon gets up and walks across the room. He pulls a stool

lot with tarot

a my pockets.

103

under him, picks up the sticks, and immediately, totally, wails away. Eyes down, arms a swift blur of movement, back bent into the urgent beat, he's gone. His music fills up every inch of the place, ricocheting off the walls, driving out the open window into the yard. After a few minutes, he wraps it up. Leaning back, he cradles the drumsticks casually in his right hand and smiles. "Okay then. Let's go. If you want, I'll show you the place where I was squatting this summer."

He takes us to an abandoned house standing alone in a field. The place is in bad shape. Built around the turn of the century, it has clearly been deserted for decades. A rickety wooden staircase missing a few boards leads upstairs to the room he used. His blankets and an old sleeping bag are still in the corner. Only jagged shards of glass remain in the large window. The stub of a candle, some stuff to read, and a little change are on the floor. Babylon gathers his belongings in his arms. "The main thing that worried me living here was that people might call the police and get me arrested. Living like this isn't as hard or as bad as everyone thinks. I don't mind it. Being warm is really nice and being able to put food in my mouth is nice, but you don't really *need* running water. You don't really *need* electricity. I knew if there was something I really needed, I could ask and people would give it to me if they had it."

Mark Brown

Some know Mark Brown as the fellow who moved up from the city twenty-five years ago to work as a care-taker on a small, neighboring island. Others met him a few years later when he and his wife Lois moved here and ran a small sawmill out behind their house. Many know him as the butcher they brought their cattle to, a man who could cut well and wouldn't charge too much.

Mark makes an impression. Maybe it's the clear eyes and warm laugh lines, or the strong, working hands, or the way he looks in his two layers of plaid flannel shirts. Maybe it's the white high tops. Could this man possibly be eighty-three?

uman. There was nothing we could do to make him go when he decided it was time to take a break.

Mark was born in 1913 in a little spot called Encampment, Wyoming. His family's place was a cattle ranch surrounded by prairie. When he was four, the family picked up and moved to Missouri. "My mom got tired of living in the hoots, and I tell you, that place was the hoots!" In the new place, still seven miles from town, the folks tried to farm sorghum cane. The family horse, Jim, pulled the buggy to town each week when the Browns took their eggs and butter to market. Mark remembers riding way high up on the seat. Jim had his favorite places to stop along the way. "I tell you, that horse was pretty near human. There was nothing we could do to make him go when he decided it was time to take a break."

Two years later the family moved west, settling on Vancouver Island in a log house with a tin roof. Mark's memories there are of the logging camp where his dad worked, of learning to eat clams, sleeping in the top bunk, and being too young to bike the fifteen miles to school each day with his brothers, Chester and Milton.

When the family moved to Seattle, they found a house on Yesler Way. His friend, the woman up the hill, always had a cookie for him. Sometimes she had men friends in too.

"'Course, I didn't know what that was about, back then." A smile plays on his lips. "I was barely a schoolboy at the time."

Mark stands by his barn, telling us the little stuff, penciling in the detail of his life. He speaks of the ups and downs, taking the bitter with the sweet. "Well, I didn't finish high school, and I say I'm not too proud of it. But I've never been on government help; I always had a job. All you have to do in this life is keep your eyes open and your mouth shut. You'll be okay." He takes his cap off for one last photograph.

What is your secret, Mark? How do you stay so young?

"Vitamins! I've been taking them since 1954. Betcha I got two to three hundred dollars worth in my cupboard at all times! That, I suppose, and the fact I don't sit down much."

Now we're in the big country kitchen, warming ourselves by the wood stove. Lois is at the counter putting finishing touches on a cherry pie. It's not often you get to see a couple who have been married sixty-three years. "If you want to know what keeps him going, it's curiosity," says Lois. There is spice and sweetness in the look she gives Mark. "My husband, he's curious about everything."

105

Corrie Haight

School children are coming to Corrie and Lark's studio to watch them blow glass, to watch them work magic. The students come as part of a visiting art class, but this is science too. The precision of the work is startling. Seconds count as the artists work with blistering heat, the furnace, and the blow rod. The sixth-graders watch, hypnotized, as Corrie and Lark blow the molten glass. In less than five minutes, a beautiful emerald bowl sits cooling. Seeing these two work together is like watching one of those 1940s movies where the couple is ballroom dancing, eyes locked, bodies moving in unison, stiletto steps perfectly timed. A tango of glassblowing.

Their studio, located in the family barn, is a hybrid

of soccer balls and exquisite Christmas ornaments, kids' castoffs and one-of-a-kind goblets, precision tools and original vases. Rainbows of handmade beads dangle in the windows. Sunlight, dancing through the beads' intense purples, greens, and blues, beams a prism on the rough barn wall. Out of all this comes artwork that sells in exclusive galleries around the country.

Corrie is the eye of the storm. Serious. Intense. Calm. We move from the heat and action of glassblowing to the quiet of her studio in the house.

Seven large, triangular windows bathe the room in soft light. An ironing board leans against the wall. Bolts of cloth, bowls of beads sorted by color, rolls of copper wire on the floor–all are touches of the artist and the woman. Along the top of a cupboard sit fifteen, maybe twenty dolls. Dolls in native clothing, dolls with braids, dolls in moccasins, dolls we 40-year-olds played with, once upon a time. Two tapestries from a Thai hill tribe hang on the wall. Corrie herself is a weaving, the threads of the woman, the business person, the mother, the wife, and the artist intertwining in a rich design.

In a family of five girls, Corrie is the middle sister. She attended several colleges, studying studio art. "My mother is an artist, a craftsperson. We were always encouraged that way. I went off to study in different places. One summer I was in Taos, studying weaving. Another time it was fiber and glass work in River Falls, Wisconsin. I was there about a year. I never lasted much at any one college. I just had to see the next place."

Corrie studied at the famous Pilchuck Glass School near Seattle when the school was in its third year. "It was a very exciting spot to be. You had artists coming from all over the world." She returned there recently to study flame-working. "It's a highly charged place, crazy and exciting. I don't like

calling myself an artist or craftsperson. I call myself a designer. I'm more comfortable with that title. Right now that means jewelry and beads, but originally I was in textile and fashion design. My favorite part is color and how colors work together. Our use of color is where we've gained attention in our work. I tend to be neutral myself. I like to blend in, not stand out."

Yes. The woman who works these intense colors into art is herself rendered in quiet hues. Corrie is finding it awkward to talk about herself or her life. She takes a breath and finds her words. "I think, as far as being part of this community, my strength is in giving to kids. It's really important for kids to learn to work with their hands instead of just bopping on a Game Boy or a computer. Our society is going so fast, it's important to slow down. I guess I think even though you may not make a living at some of these crafts, it's important for kids, for people, to have these opportunities in their lives. Like leather-making. I love to make leather shoes. It's not economically feasible to make them, but you just love the thought that you can do it! Or like sewing, to take something flat and make it three-dimensional, to me it's magic. Kids need to know they can make things with their hands, that they can develop the ability, whether or not they choose to use it later in their lives.

"I think we humans are curious. We all want to know what makes each other tick. It's the anticipation of something different happening each day that gets me up in the morning. Who knows what the day will bring, especially with children?

"To me, the meaning of life is definitely family and friends. People. I hope I've inspired some people to work with their hands. I would like to see some traditions saved, revived, for their beauty more than anything. I guess that's something I'd like to leave behind."

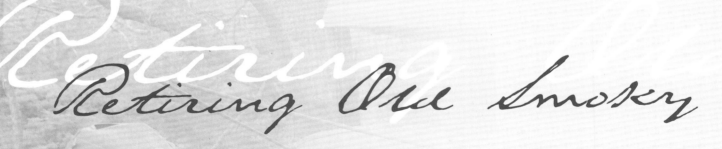

Retiring Old Smoky

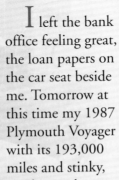

I left the bank office feeling great, the loan papers on the car seat beside me. Tomorrow at this time my 1987 Plymouth Voyager with its 193,000 miles and stinky, smoking exhaust would be officially retired, and I'd be the new owner of Susan's 1989, low-mileage, mint-condition Volvo.

Driving to my friend Liz's, I found myself following a red station wagon doing about ten miles under the limit. I could see an older woman behind the wheel. Two large dogs rode shotgun, their heads out the passenger window. After a few blocks she slowed down even more. Maybe she was a tourist. When we got by the lake, I pulled out to pass.

Halfway around, I glanced over. The woman looked straight at me, a thunderous expression on her face, and shot a big gesture out the window with her left hand.

Although there was no profanity, it was high on meaning.

Now, I have to stop here to tell you that even in this peaceful place, that woman scared me. I have plenty of friends in the city with stories of wackos and road rage. When I looked in my rearview mirror and saw her arm still out the window pumping up and down, I felt my adrenaline kick in and heard a little warning bell go off in my brain.

I stepped on the gas to put some distance between us. Through the haze of my Plymouth's rude exhaust, I watched the woman fade back. Wheeling quickly into Liz's driveway, I hoped that, like a grizzly after an innocent hiker, she'd lose my scent and blow on past.

She pulled right in behind me.

My joyful mood now totally destroyed, I opened my car door to deal with the kook. My mind was racing, replaying the last few minutes, trying desperately to fathom what I could have done to tick this stranger off. I tried to remember my Zen training–take a breath, relax, breathe–but as I walked back to her car, my mind was buzzing like a hornet's nest with a stick jabbed in it.

She leaned out the window, red-faced, as I walked up.

"Your car is smoking, dear! This could be dangerous! Is there some way I can help?" My iced-up distrust melted in a puddle of relief. What I'd taken for anger, I saw instantly, was her own fear–for *my* safety.

Seeing no emergency, the woman launched into a quick explanation. "Thirty years ago when I was living on the mainland, there was a lady driving along whose car was smoking just about as bad as yours. As I

watched, it burst into flames. She was so petrified she couldn't move. I had to pull her out of that burning car myself. Today when I saw you I thought, 'This can't be happening again.'"

My mood now totally restored, I told her about my car purchase, about my plans to retire Old Smoky tomorrow, and, a little sheepishly, about trying to ditch her.

Her eyes crinkled at the corners as she laughed at my confession. "Road rage? Oh honey, not here on the island! Never. We're family out here, more or less. We care about one another. We look after each other. That's what living here is about. Are you a newcomer?"

I extended my hand through her window and introduced myself. "I'm Linda Leamer," she said. "I live right down the road with my husband. I'll tell you a little story about this place. When we were first married, thirty years ago, we went out for a ride on the island one night. There was a beautiful August moon, huge and golden, you know the kind I mean. We stopped along the side of the road to enjoy it together. Well, no fewer than four cars stopped to see if we needed help! 'Sure you can help,' we told them all. 'Sit awhile, and help us look at the moon!'"

Debbie Hayward

ward

"I am such a shy person," Debbie begins. She sips her tea quietly. A fanciful Chinese dragon dances around the blue and white bowl of the steaming mug. She looks up. A half-smile lights her face. Her eyes dip back to the tea.

Being with Debbie is a little like being with a deer in the forest. Quiet. Safe. There's a feeling of the abundance of time.

It's difficult to begin our conversation, knowing this woman's history. Her young son died in a tractor accident, and later, a car wreck left her daughter paralyzed.

"Life kind of makes you want to put on a crash helmet every so often," Debbie says, letting her brown eyes connect deeply. "But it's amazing how enduring the heart is. I continue to think a lot about it, wondering about the energy that keeps us moving, keeps us breathing, allowing us to live from the heart despite our pain and suffering."

Rishi, her son, was born first. Her daughter H'Sien (pronounced Shen), came a year and a half later. Could Debbie tell about their names? "Rishi has this sense of a teacher with access to the unlimited, to pure wisdom. H'Sien comes from a collection of wonderful, wild Chinese stories by Chuang Tzu. It's the name of a character who embodies amazing wisdom and a tremendous sense of humor."

The conversation turns to the children's accidents. I ask a question, using the word "catastrophe." Debbie gently reframes my sentence before continuing. "I wouldn't use that word, 'catastrophe.' To me those things were more like unfoldings. It's commonplace these days to say that reality is as we perceive it, each of us creating our own world in a way. What's true for me is that the events in this life are neither good nor bad, hard or easy in themselves; it's just how we choose to see them.

"Rishi's death was a numbing experience; the pain was excruciating. In retrospect I can find a lot of gifts from that time, although I couldn't see them then. I remember I used to wonder what even got me out of bed in the morning. Afterwards came a period of pulling in, closing others out. It was part of my work to be accepting of his death and to know it as part of the path we are all on, to try to understand how we human beings can experience such pain and still keep going. To explore that life force inside of us."

Within a few years Debbie and her husband separated, then divorced.

H'Sien, a 4.0 student and an avid athlete excelling in distance running, was in Hawaii for her junior year of high school when she had her car accident. Debbie and her former husband flew to Honolulu, arriving to find their daughter in a coma, her body paralyzed from the chest down. She was sixteen.

Debbie talks about a transformational experience at H'Sien's bedside. "Suddenly there was a breaking-through. The light that has always existed was just *there*. I felt filled with love for this little piece of broken body on the bed who was my daughter. It involved nothing more than understanding the underlying essence behind our daily experience. The event was a major clarification and realization for me. It was about change being inevitable, how it is to be welcomed, as every moment is to be welcomed. I realized very clearly that these situations are opportunities to grow, if we choose to see them that way. I hope I'll always make that choice, to see these things as gifts, to let them move me beyond my boundaries.

111

There was an amazing invisible net of people, angels in living form really,

who showered

"They say when you're ready for understanding, a leaf can fall and you'll open or," laughing now, "if you're not ripe, a tree could fall on your head and nothing would happen! In my case this awareness came partly through the act of surrender and partly by being completely hit over the head."

She tells more about being at her daughter's bedside during the ten days of H'Sien's coma. "I've never really prayed, but I found myself asking to let the energy of the universe flow through me so I could be of the greatest help. And I felt very supported. I can't really put words to it." Debbie pauses. "Sometimes, of course, I was in a different place, with fear, just wondering how to get through this mentally and emotionally.

"H'Sien's accident, coming just eight years after Rishi's death, took me back to the question 'What is this force that leads us through life?' Understanding came roaring to the surface for me, the realization that living a life of love is why we're here. With it came the desire to be free from all the pettiness, from anything and everything that restricts our access to our inner divinity.

"H'Sien chose to see her situation as a great gift and a blessing, to move on from there. Of course, some of the nurses wanted to label that thinking denial and repression. One nurse took me aside and asked me not to give my daughter misplaced encouragement, false hope. She wanted us to see the tragedy of H'Sien becoming a paraplegic. We felt the pain and the loss of her accident, but nonetheless there was this constant inner urging to see the gift and the blessing as H'Sien moved from one state of ability to another.

"H'Sien never hesitates to let people know she is in her wheelchair temporarily. She doesn't know the process or type of intervention that will come, but she knows it will. She sees her accident as this tremendous opportunity for reha-bilitation of her spirit as well as her body.

"There was an amazing invisible net of people, angels in living form really, who showered us with their blessings …people in the hospital, a person on the airplane coming home, just everywhere. We entered into this universe of omniscient love and grace. We recognized it in those we came into contact with. Learning to open to it was part of our curriculum as we knew it then."

One of those angels was a nurse in the hospital who introduced them to the teachings of Gurumayi, a spiritual teacher from India living in the West. "There it was again, that karmic unfolding. Such a great blessing. Gurumayi embraces all religious thought, honoring the tenets shared by all faiths. She is considered to reside in a fully enlightened state. Both H'Sien and I have become her students."

H'Sien, now twenty-one, is a junior at Stanford University studying pre-med. "She is drawn to psychiatry and what you might call the enabling process, helping people move beyond their limitations. She is interested in the work of Deepak Chopra. They met at his Center for Well Being in La Jolla, and she has worked there as part of her studies.

"One thing that comes to mind through Rishi's death and H'Sien's accident is the tremendous community support and outpouring of love we received from people on this island. Those experiences brought us into this community in ways that we normally wouldn't have been. There's no one who hasn't been touched in some way by tragedy, and being able to share with the heart has been the gift. I have this feeling I want to repay it. Finding a means of doing that is a motivating task. Choosing to volunteer with hospice is part of that, the opportunity to live this life with service, with love. For me it's also learning about detachment from results–doing the work for love itself, because whatever needs doing, simply needs doing.

"I have a longing to know God. It seems to grow and

·ith their blessings…

grow in me. I want to live in that state of realization, that greatest joy. All we are here for is to live in a state of love. This is the perfect time, the perfect place, right now, to do it. But remaining there is not always easy! There are the bills to pay. It's all part of the work, and it fills each day with so much joy."

Debbie talks softly but with exuberant energy. She is sure-footed in places many of us tiptoe. My pen, zooming across the pad, can't possibly keep up. I ask her to slow for a moment and repeat a thought. She laughs, caught off-guard by the difficulty of catching and restating her idea. Once her words are out, they seem to be off on their own. "It's about trust, I suppose, not being too attached to things, even our own ideas."

She talks about her work as owner of the Green Dragon Nursery. "It's an interesting experience to often feel such love for the person across the counter, maybe the person I'm selling petunias to! It's ecstatic, delicious! You feel like you want to take each and every one home, shower them with affection. Of course our society doesn't have a form to express or even condone that; there isn't really an appropriate way. It's a love which may not be understood. So for me, basically a very shy person, the feelings come out quietly. If I were more verbal, they might come bubbling out.

"We see ourselves as these separate entities. It's separateness from one another that causes some problems. Often, in our culture especially, we go to 'Somebodyness School,' starting early with limitations of who we think we are. I actually feel we're enrolled from the day we're born. Our teachers don't seem to know anything else. It's really not until we learn to be nobody that we gain access to our real potential, our divinity. To me that's what life is all about, to be free of the ego which tries to define what we should be, who we are, what we need. After all, we are each God in many different costumes. It's delightful.

"The essence, I guess, is realizing I'm just God's energy in this form. It's by way of spiritual practice that I work on remembering that. I surround myself with pictures of Gurumayi and devote a certain portion of every day to meditation and studying the teachings. But also it comes from seeing a sparkle in someone's eye, a smile coming from the heart. You suddenly realize 'There it is again! How could I have forgotten?' And you remind yourself to see yourself in others, to know we're all the same Self, capital S. In fact it's the small self, the ego, we're here to learn about and surrender. I have this sense of infinite gratitude for having any insight at all, for this path, and for being able to share this with others with an increasingly open heart."

113

Lynn T. Waller

It's a cold winter night at the old Grange Hall. The Island Storytellers are finishing up a fine evening performance of tales, part of an island-wide effort to raise funds to build our first Community Center. The stage goes dark, and from the wings Cynthia Dilling–dressed as a man in jacket, slacks, vest, and hat–struts slowly, impressively on stage. "Hi," she drawls, eying the crowd. "My name is Lynn Waller!" Heads swivel in the little room to find the real Lynn sitting in the audience. His bewilderment turns to surprise, then he throws his head back with a booming laugh.

Months later we meet Lynn, chairman of the Community Center Board during its $1.5 million fund-raising drive, for a visit in his backyard. Clasping his hands behind his head, he takes a deep breath and tips his deck chair back to a comfortable angle. He closes his eyes. Summer looks good on this man. As he crosses his legs, bright turquoise socks pop out above heavy work boots. Across a wide expanse of green lawn, an American flag, high up a flagpole, snaps in the wind.

This morning Lynn has been telling his own stories, richly detailing his years as principal of the award-winning Shorecrest High School near Seattle, the central place of marriage, faith, and family in his life, the advanced degrees he attained, his thirty-six years in public education, and his national role in education leadership. Lynn has an amazing memory for detail. He liberally seasons the conversation with exact events, dates, and names that pinpoint particulars spanning over fifty years.

Lynn was taught the values of service and responsibility at a young age…and they took. "My folks provided my brothers and me with lots of opportunities to develop our own selfhood. They were always fostering leadership situations for us. All three of us were student body presidents. From the age of fourteen, I was going to two-month summer camp. In 1938 it was Camp

Wigwasati in northern Ontario. I learned to sail, swim, canoe, and sleep outside. Gosh, we got tough as nails!

"I've always had a service orientation. It came to fruition in classroom teaching and developed into education leadership. I participated in opening four secondary schools. That was a tremendously creative experience for me. But you know, I still don't know what my talents are. I guess you could say I'm what they call a gifted generalist. Would I do what I've done over again? You bet! I don't have any regrets in life. I would say another thing too. When you look at it, I've had a very fortunate life, but I've had failures also. Remember, failures are an opportunity to learn about yourself, and from them I've gained a great deal.

"Both my wife Marlys and I keep going like there's no tomorrow. I tell my kids I'm going to live to be one hundred and nine, and they shake their heads. 'Would you really like to live so long?' they ask me. Yeah! I'd like to do that. But I'll be candid, I want a little more quiet now. I want time to sit out here." He sweeps his arm past the porch to the water and islands beyond. "I enjoy splitting firewood and mowing the lawn. I want to get back to reading some philosophy. You know at this age

…well, I don't wish for a moment to sound morbid, but we've had some fine folks leave us lately. Not too long ago my son said to me, 'Dad, you're seventy-five now; you're in your last quarter!'" Another generous laugh. "I will say, at this age we begin to feel our own mortality. I'm not afraid to die, but I'd like it to be peaceful when I go. Hey, I'd like to be sitting out here, and just…go away. You know, that would be wonderful.

"What I want to say is that some of the most important things I've learned in my life have come through my kids' generation: acceptance, tolerance, and patience. This island has a strong threshold for tolerance and alternative lifestyles. It's utterly amazing—and one of the reasons why living here is such a delight! I tell you, intolerance puts a real burr under my saddle!

"I think if you talked to our children they would say neither Marlys nor I lectured about values; we lived them. A little formula I believe in is 'Discipline + Responsibility = Freedom.' We all want to be free to do what we want. In order for that to happen, there are two cardinal things to accept. The first is discipline. You can't be free without it. I use music, art, or athletics as examples here. You can never be great in any field without putting in a lot of effort, and that means putting discipline first. The other part is responsibility. Once you make a decision, you abide by it and live with the consequences. If you don't, you won't have freedom."

Lynn moves on to another favorite theme, family. "Marlys and I got married the day after Christmas, 1950. It's been a lot of fun, a heck of a lot of fun! But you gotta understand, this is a partnership with this woman I'm married to. I've always had great respect for my wife. We have great love for each other."

How would you like to be remembered?

"I really never thought about that," he says, giving himself time to reflect on the question. "The comment was made at my school that I was a very caring person. I'm not a hero or anything. I've been lucky. I married a great gal, had four great kids and ten grandkids." He pauses. "I don't know that I've answered your question, though." Very quiet now, almost under his breath, "I was a good guy." It's a somber moment, the words said so softly. After a moment, I repeat them back to him. "Yes, that's what I said," Lynn answers gently. "When I'm gone, I hope people will say I was a good guy."

This island has a strong threshold for tolerance and alternative lifestyles . . . I tell you, intolerance puts a real burr under my saddle!

Marie Van Erp

Annie's doctor appointment was delayed, so she stepped outside the clinic to have a cigarette. She was taking a comforting drag off her Old Gold when a tall, handsomely dressed woman came out the door. Fixing Annie with a serious look, she pointed her cane directly at her. "I'm going to die!"

Totally disarmed, Annie could only look at her. "Oh, I'm so sorry."

"Do you know WHY I'm going to die?" the woman demanded. Generally very self-assured, Annie shook her head meekly. Who was this stranger with the beautiful, chocolate-brown eyes?

"I'm going to die because I smoked. I have emphysema!" The woman's cane stabbed the air for punctuation. "Cigarettes are terrible. Many good people are already dead because they weren't told. They didn't know. Now YOU know. You should quit immediately. No further excuses!"

Telling the story, Annie, forty-two, said that even though it was jarring to hear someone address her like that, there was a gift in it. It's rare for a person to step forward to offer real help, she explained. Usually we are too afraid of rejection to take the risk.

There's a new term in our society for the ability to see and ignore the everyday crises and pain in each other's lives: "compassion fatigue." Clarie Van Erp, Annie's champion that day, clearly didn't have that problem.

Sitting in Clarie's garden some weeks later, I ask about the meaning of life, what gives purpose and joy to her days. "Today I don't care! Look there." Her cane guides my gaze. "The caterpillars are all over my trees. Where will my apples come from? I may have to call the market and have some delivered." Clarie makes it sound like a curse, having apples *delivered.*

"I don't know what I really think," she softens. "I change my mind. What bugs me is how many people there are who don't give a damn about anyone else. Some people on this island just give, give, give. Some take, take, take. My father was a lay minister, a top Bible student. I was taught from the very beginning to think about others.

"I want to be remembered as being very kind, because I am. A lot of people don't know that about me. Why not? I haven't told them!" A raspy laugh completes her sentence. "I want to give, but I want credit for it. I'm not like some of these women who work with babies and get no credit."

Clarie, seventy-seven, talks about her life in the theater. It's her touchstone, the place all her conversations go, no matter where they begin. She tells about helping start the Country Playhouse Theater in Houston forty years ago, her favorite roles as an actress, her work with movie stars, the plays she directed. "Folks still call for advice, asking me which script to use, which director to hire," she says.

The actress in her, the storyteller, takes center stage again. She tucks a wisp of hair behind her ear and continues. "As long as I can remember, I've gotten a kick out of where I was, whether watching a beaver build a dam, working in the hospital, exhibition diving off a sixteen-foot board, or teaching school. Do you want to pick that shell up? I collected it in Fiji. Did I mention I'm a collector?"

Clarie collects collections. Her house and barn are stuffed with stuff, amazing collections of exotic seashells, fabrics, sculpture, books, evening bags, furniture, pillows. She's outfitted one entire porch with rows of shelves to handle hundreds of jars of her homemade chutney, jam, and garden vegetables. A quick check of label dates shows that this is a vintage collection; many jars are from the 1980s.

Our conversation comes full circle, back to that day at the clinic. "I don't want to die. I've got too many things I want to do." My eyes go involuntarily to the portable oxygen canister Clarie keeps with her today. Her breathing is labored at times. Her comments are matter-of-fact, no self-pity. "I don't know the purpose of life, but I sure know I wouldn't want to miss out on it." Dipping her chin dramatically, she looks over her glasses. "We've been put here by God for some reason, but *by God* I don't know what it is! When I think of why we're here, I'll let you know."

Maybe we should ask Annie.

119

Robert Herrmann

Robert meets us at the door in sweater, slacks, and his trademark yellow clogs. The tone of his home is set by his collection of original artwork: a kimono with arms outstretched in classic Japanese style on the dining room wall, commissioned stained glass over the door, a pastel triptych above the mantle, a dramatically lighted goddess amulet, a couch upholstered in burgundy tapestry. "Into what shape will you mold the raw matter of your life?" asks script on a glass globe on the buffet.

Robert begins, almost immediately, with a story about his grandparents in Hitler's camps. They were Czechoslovakian Jews. It was the early 1930s, a time when war was still a rumbling, a rumor in Europe. Wanting their son, Robert's father, safe, they sent him to attend Columbia University in the States. When the war came and German troops crashed into their town of Pilsen, Robert's grandparents and all the family were taken off. They died in the camps. Every one. "That included my grandmother, Anna. According to family stories, she was called the Angel of Auschwitz. She led the Jewish women of Pilsen into the gas chambers singing the Czech national anthem. I still have some of the postcards

they sent from the camps—you know, the ones the Germans made them send saying everything was fine, that they were getting plenty to eat."

Years later, a package was delivered to Robert's father in America. Inside were jewelry and family pieces, his mother's and father's things from their life before the camps. How they were smuggled out and where they'd been all those years is still a mystery.

This story tumbles out of Robert in the first few minutes, even before we sit down. Now he offers steaming cups of jasmine tea in the living room. Perched with the birds high on a bluff over Hunter Bay, Robert's home is his nest, his womb, his showplace. It is the sanctuary he shares with his partner, Ron. "We go outside on the deck even when it's dreary. It's ever-changing, this view! Well, look at it! It's never boring, never in stasis. Just look at the light and patterns on the water. It's subtle here; it seeps into you.

"Max. Come here, boy!" Robert pats his thigh, and a gray-nosed black lab appears like magic, paws making a fine click-click on the hardwood. Old friends.

Robert continues, shifting to his own history now. At age seventeen he had a lead in the National Touring Company's production of the Broadway hit musical *Hair*. "It was 1971,

121

Robaert Herrmann

I was raised with the rules. Always buy white appliances. Always put your napkin in your lap. Always be on time. I'm, like total

I was a junior in high school, and they offered me $500 a week! I think my mother was worried about me dropping out of high school to do it, but she said, 'If this is what you want to do, I will buy you the luggage.' And she did. It was horrid stuff! A deep rust color, hideous, really ca-ca. Remember those sets?" Arms thrown up in mock horror, he gives an exaggerated shrug.

"My mother was a guiding force in my life. She was just four foot, eight inches tall, ninety pounds, a total powerhouse! She died in my arms at Marin General Hospital, just down the hall from the room where I was born." He talks quietly about that day. "I got this flash of me coming into the world, my mother holding me in her arms. And then, here we were again, this time she was in my arms, going out of the world. She was seventy-four.

"I have to believe that we're not created to be here just once. I can't believe you get to be with people you love once and never again. Why would we go through all the work of developing these relationships to have it all just…gone? No, I don't believe that anymore. I feel like those we love who have passed on are watching, still very much part of us in a metaphysical way. They're always around, either inside or outside of us.

"What I learned about loss is that we tend to want to move through it really quickly. But I think what's critical is to stay in that in-between space as long as it takes, and it can take a while. The truth is there is no right or wrong way when you're talking about grieving. Nobody has the right to tell you to get over your grief, to get on with your life. At a time of loss, you just hope to have people around you who love you. You hope they won't stay away out of their own perceived awkwardness.

"I pray a lot. I don't pray to God because I don't know if I believe in God as a person, but I do believe there is a universal energy that flows. I almost always pray for clarity. Isn't that what it's all about? The most important thing to remember is that the universe is absolutely clear. It gives you exactly what you ask for. So you have to be careful! For me life is also about having faith that you'll be provided for, whatever you need to learn. I believe that. But you know, sometimes I forget. Don't we all? Don't we *always*? It's like, 'Helllooooooo!' But by the end of the day I usually remember to ask myself 'What's the lesson here?'" Robert is laughing now. "Sometimes the universe just keeps hitting us on the head, over and over, with the same bat!

"There's a wonderful thought, I'm paraphrasing here, something like 'When you come to the end of all the light you know and you're about to step out into the darkness, you have to trust that one of two things will happen: someone will be there to catch you when you fall, or you will learn to fly.'

"One of the things my parents taught me is that you can attain your dreams. You don't have to die with regret. I believe, as my dad did, that life is juicy! What's the point of living, otherwise? I was raised with the rules. Always buy white appliances. Always put your napkin in your lap. Always be on time. I'm, like *totally*, into Miss Manners! For me, another thing has been to try to live without fear of censure. There can be boundaries, of course, but you don't have to conform! It's okay to wear those yellow shoes. It's all about living a succulent life, loving what you do to the nth degree. I don't know if it's cultural or universal, but we're not necessarily taught to follow our passion.

"Now my father, he was a wild man. Amazing! His passion was painting." During the school year, life for Robert and his two brothers revolved around his parents' careers as founders of a large chain of children's retail stores. When summer came, the family tent-camped Europe from

...to Miss Manners!

Amsterdam to the island of Ibiza off the coast of Spain.

Robert's public persona is bubbly, bouncy, exuberant, all-over-the-place energy. People know him as a straight shooter, a man who may not sandpaper off the rough edges of his remarks. He talks about struggling with his own willingness to be blunt. "I am hypercritical of people and of life. I don't suffer fools easily. I don't like stupidity. It can be very hurtful to be that direct, but sometimes life's too short not to say what you need to say. Sometimes I realize later on that I didn't have to say something. But I did say it. Was it to make myself feel bigger or better or brighter? The cost, the expense of doing that is to yourself. You give your own power away by being smaller, less that you need to be. I think you get your truest sense of self by being responsible for your mistakes.

"Gossip intrigues me. I've been busted on that one before, let me tell ya! But I also think gossip is one way a community connects. There is good gossip and bad gossip. The good connects us. When you live in a community that is bound by water, you can't just get angry and turn away.

Here people will leave you alone, but if you're in trouble it is truly miraculous. People are there when you need them; they just turn out for you. It crosses all boundaries. My whole point is to say it's a diverse community. It's safe to be who you are here."

He talks about being part of a same-sex couple. "Being gay is completely cellular, it's a non-topic for me. One is born gay. There is no question about it. Almost everyone I know can trace feelings way, way back. Why would a person choose to be a second-class citizen? But I don't think people have to suffer from anything. You only suffer if you're a victim. I learned that from friends dying of AIDS.

"It's like I'm a work in progress. I don't know that we ever get to be finished. I don't mean to sound smarmy, but you just get to be who you are, at the moment and in the moment. And that changes. The only thing you own is your word. If you abuse that, how can you move through the world? Here's what I believe in: Be who you are. Do what you do. Honor your work and your world."

123

Saying Goodbye

They held Sally Bill's memorial in her sheep pasture, forty wide-open acres under the arch of sky she loved. In a winter notorious for wind, rain, and cold, her day arrived cool and gray with a little drizzle—weather we native Northwesterners secretly adore. Like one of Sally's own handwoven shawls, it held us close and warm.

Prayer flags marked the way up the hill and across the field where a huge white tent was raised. Family and friends had worked hard spreading straw for walkways across the rain-soaked ground, placing hundreds of hay bales inside for seating, tying graceful branches and boughs to the metal tent poles, making an altar of sorts up front.

It was somber, entering the tent. Probably 350 people were already there. Taking a spot along the side, I looked at the little handout. "In Celebration of the Life of Sally Bill." Sally's photo was on the front, her face a tapestry of wrinkles, a wonderful weaving of laugh lines and twinkles around the eyes. In the picture, she wore a work shirt. Most of us dressed that same way for the service—fresh jeans, a nice sweater, a raincoat just in case. I turned to the back page. "Sally Bill: mother, gardener, weaver, sheep farmer, baker, organizer of community celebrations." Twenty-three lines of serendipity followed. "Last known height: 5 feet. Estimated diaper changes of her six children over thirteen years: 45,000.

Last words: 'I know I'm okay.'
Estimated nights sleeping in the
barn during lambing season: 200.
Number of plastic knees: 2.
Graduated Vassar College in 1941.
Bought the John Deere tractor
as a Christmas present for herself
in 1983."

At the front of the tent, a handmade wooden pallet rested on a hay bale, its center section secured to a pair of lean poles about seven feet long. Draped with a beautiful cloth, it held the box of Sally's ashes plus flowers, notes, keepsakes, and mementos from family and friends.

Looking around I saw neighbors, strangers, folks up from the city, and children, lots of children. Here on the island, children come to weddings, funerals, potlucks, parties, and gatherings of all kinds. They hold an important place in the circle of community. I remember how strange that seemed when I moved here: seeing mothers nursing babies, little ones napping on a lap, wiggly preschoolers attending these events. Here if children are fidgety during a long event, they get down, roam around, and let their wiggles out. A few giggles may come, a little ruckus might erupt, a toddler might even wander up front. It makes people smile.

The minister, a friend to many, opened the service by asking us to stand, join hands, and sing a hymn. Three of Sally's friends accompanied us on cello, violin, and mandolin, lifting their tender notes above our own. Palm to palm with the people next to me, my throat went tight, my eyes wet, my heart full.

Each of Sally's children spoke during the service. A group of friends sang. Neighbors rose to tell stories, read poems, and offer their gratitude.

After about two hours, Sally's grandchildren came forward and, lifting the pallet, led us in a procession outdoors. Earlier in the day, they had prepared a bonfire the old-fashioned way, rubbing sticks together until cedar sparked, flame jumped, and the mountain of drift logs began to burn. Now the pyre glowed red. Carefully the grandchildren placed the pallet on top.

It was a holy moment, ashes to ashes. Baskets filled with small cedar branches passed from hand to hand around the circle. I took a fragrant bough and, saying a prayer, stepped close, adding it to the flames.

As the smoke rose, our songs did too…gospels, hymns, family favorites. "How about the Hokey Pokey?" came a suggestion. While some laughed and some cried, the whole circle of us put our right foot in and our right foot out. We danced goodbye to Sally.

The next day winter returned. Wind shouldered open the flaps of the empty tent and, picking the giant canvas up, tossed it high. A white handkerchief now, it waved like a silent, departing friend, then settled down upon Sally's field. The straw, which had marked our path, the wind took in wild hands and scattered to the four directions.

Andy Holland

"I was all alone, facing death, and I was scared. Stationed high in a Forest Service lookout on Miners Ridge, twenty miles from the nearest human being, I wondered if I could survive the night. The pain was getting worse and I had almost reached the point of a merciful blackout. One by one the stars, which had seemed permanently fixed in the sky-canopy, disappeared. Suddenly, a light that I had not seen before appeared in the eastern sky–a beacon with the magnitude of Venus in December, that grew brighter and brighter. 'My God!' I breathed. 'This must be it, the amazing light that only a prospective emigrant from Earth could perceive.' I lost all sense of fear and pain, and a feeling of euphoria and resignation pervaded my whole being while I prayed and waited expectantly for the end. To die, all alone, was not the catastrophe that I had always imagined. Now it seemed clear that the human body had miraculous adaptations for death, the same as it had for life."

Switchbacks
by Andy Holland

So begins Andy Holland's memoir about his adventures in the U.S. Forest Service. His solitary struggle that night of July 1, 1932, continued when he concocted a makeshift ice bag from a waxed paper Rye Krisp box liner and filled it with snow and table salt. Placing it on his swollen side, he collapsed on the bed. By morning the pain was bearable. In a few days Andy decided he could complete his two-month solo assignment in the remote lookout. After Andy hiked out, his doctor operated and found evidence of arrested gangrene when he removed the appendix. "The salted snow had done the trick by freezing the infected organ, but it was a close call."

Andy loves to tell stories.

He weaves another. I lean forward, wondering how this one turns out. Andy and his wife Dolly are in a remote part of the Glacier Peak wilderness when they're charged by a grizzly. He tells Dolly to climb a tree, but she won't go, so they turn tail and scramble through a grove of alpine fir, "with that bear crashing along behind us." Running flat-out, they take a fast turn to throw the huge animal off their trail. It works. "Bears have a keen sense of smell, but they can't see very well. Dolly said if we could have gotten out of the mountains that night she'd never go back in." Andy throws his head back and laughs. "Of course she did. We had many more adventures together in the mountains. That grizzly

really scared her though. She said I swore at him, but I don't think I did!"

Andy might, if pressed, describe his life with a list that includes high school and college teacher, author, traveler, baseball coach, semipro pitcher, Forest Service lookout, and adventurer. Friends would add philanthropist, gentleman, and gentle man. In Japan they designate certain beloved elders as "living national treasures." Our community has an uncommon number of people who might be given that title, and Andy is one.

Today he's wearing gray slacks, a pale blue dress shirt, and shined wingtips. His white hair, parted on the left, combs into a deep natural wave. It's not until he walks to the kitchen to make a fresh pot of coffee that his body tells its age. He is careful. A recent fall gave him trouble. "Yes, I'm almost eighty-nine. I've often said, 'Gee, to be eighty again!'" His bright blue eyes are twinkling. Coming back to the living room he offers two steaming cups. One says Damn I'm Good!; the other, Hell, I'm Better!

"What's important to me are the simple things in life, like meeting people, making friendships around the world, and traveling. Of course, we both loved to travel and meet people of all nations. That does away with hatred as far as I'm concerned. We never ran into any nasty people, except some of our own. Dolly and I traveled all over the world

except Siberia and Antarctica. New Guinea, Australia, Africa, Machu Pichu, the Galapagos Islands, and India were special places for us. In Pakistan we went far back into the mountains where the Hunzas live. They're the oldest people in the world." He pulls up short. "I'm a little worried that I'm doing some bragging here. I don't want that! I just want to express the miracles in my life."

We spend a few minutes walking through the apartment, looking at framed photos he took during their travels: two tribeswomen in Kenya intently watching a Polaroid photograph develop, and a breathtaking high mountain shot in western China. Back in the living room, Andy launches into a story about his childhood. Once, while playing in the woods, he took a bad fall, smashing his left elbow. The local doctor couldn't repair it. "The best he could do was wrap it in hot towels. I lay in the hospital for six weeks. I was just seven years old at the time. It was 1918, during the first World War, and Dr. Moures, evidently one of the best bone surgeons in the country, happened to be visiting the local Naval shipyard. They contacted him and he operated, wiring my arm back together in a demonstration for twenty-two doctors."

Smiling, Andy flexes his left arm. "Of course, some of the smaller bones are missing." He stretches both arms out, showing that his left is considerably shorter. His right became his pitching arm. "Oh golly, I *lived* baseball, playing from grade school right on through college. You know, that doctor died in the 1918 flu epidemic, just three weeks after he operated on me. Talk about miracles, I've had 'em!

"My parents died when I was in grade school, so I had to make my own way. For two years my uncle stayed with us three children. After that I lived with my older sister until I finished high school. It was kind of tough, but one learns to cope with so many situations when you have to fight your own way through. You can make your own way in life if you put your heart and soul into it. When I started out, I didn't have a hill of beans, but if you save and work you can make a good life." He tells about getting a scholarship at Washington State University and later transferring to the University of Washington to study forestry.

A college friend there told Andy he had a sister who would be in town for the weekend. They were having a dance. "Dolly, well, that's another miracle. What is that song, 'Some Enchanted Evening'? Yes, we hit it off right away!" The two had fifty-five years of marriage. She passed on a few years ago. "My wife was just a wonderful ambassador. We hoped to create this feeling of friendship wherever we traveled."

Do you have any advice to offer?

"Advice? By golly, that's a tough one! I don't think I'm all that wise." Tipping back in his recliner, he quietly considers the question. Then he leans forward. "Save money to travel. You know, people used to ask us how in the world we paid for those trips. At the time I was teaching high school, earning $100 a month and selling shoes on Saturday. That was Depression times. We knew people who would smoke two packs a day and have two drinks at night. We calculated how much it would cost us to finance the same habit, then took that amount of money and earmarked it for travel. If you do the math, you'll see that the same idea would work today. In just a few years, a person could have a trip around the world. I'd like to persuade young people to try that plan. It could save their health, stimulate them in their studies, and affect their lives in so many ways."

The conversation returns to that night at the lookout. "Now I have no fear of dying at all," Andy says, as he goes to the bookshelf. "I have a wonderful philosophy book here

called *Human Destiny*. I think it's impossible not to believe in God when one studies astronomy and sees how the universe operates by laws. The older one gets, the more amazed one becomes at how the body works and how life adapts. I believe that man was created in the image of God spiritually, not physically. God doesn't eat breakfast! It's in the *spirit* that we're in alignment with God."

Andy thumbs through another book to a section documenting plants' response to human thought. He eagerly points to the data charts. "See how this line spikes when the scientist communicates positively with the plant? And look what happens when the plant's leaf is cut. That'll make you think twice before you prune your trees! I'm interested in clairvoyance, telepathy, and other phenomena. I think a person should keep an open mind.

"I believe we're all broadcasters in a way, in thoughts, not words. I think prayer might be in that same category; that it is our Internet with God. Prayer is a very real thing, but you can't record it on a machine. There's something in the spirit that picks it up. There's so much we humans don't know, limited as we are by our five senses. In some ways, we're about like frogs trying to understand calculus."

Yes, I'm almost eighty-nine. I've often said,
'Gee, to be eighty again!'

I like to think I'm not materialist

Serina Adams

Serina and Clara, the family's golden retriever, are playing together on the front grass. The pup is bounding around, all wiggles and joy. "Clara! Clara! Give me that ball," Serina calls, clearly delighted with the game.

This young woman's life could be described with words that tell of a connected family, beautiful home, artistically talented parents, academic excellence, and athletic accomplishment. But Serina would be uncomfortable with that. Perhaps it is the artist in her that chooses to color her experience in muted tones.

"I don't believe you should put a label on people," she says. "We can be different things all at once. It's too easy to put people in little boxes. We're more dimensional than that. I think judging others is too limiting." She stops, smiling a little now. "But people do want to know who you are. Sometimes you *have to* describe yourself..." She leaves the thought there, accepting the ambiguity.

think if all my stuff went away I'd still be okay.

Inside, Serina shows us her room. It's a small space, a converted closet tucked under the rafters on the second floor, with a bed, a bookshelf, a little cupboard doubling as a table, and an antique washstand. "A good place to hear the rain," she says. "I love the rain! It always makes me feel better. When I wake up and hear it on the roof, I think, 'Oh, it's raining; it's going to be a good day.'" There are touches of the child, the teen, and the woman here. Tedward, her much-mended teddy bear, sits on the bed. Her first handmade batik scarf drapes on the wall. The family kitty, Simonian, snoozes on the pillow.

Her closet, open to the room, holds less than you'd expect for an eighteen-year-old. "I like to think I'm not materialistic, to think if all my stuff went away I'd still be okay, I'd still be me. I just want to have what I need. I'm always cleaning out. I kind of like that idea, getting rid of things society wants us to have. It's sort of a balance, though. We need some of those things. It's a little like being polite, you know, like asking how is the weather, or smiling when you don't feel like it. It's just necessary sometimes."

Downstairs now, Serina sits at the old oak kitchen table. Beyond the leaded-glass window, green fields stretch toward the tree line. Light rain begins to fall. "One of the things I do is use writing to help me understand my own jumble. I write because sometimes it's hard for others to understand me." Serina tells about a little box she's had for years, a special box. She writes her ideas on origami-style papers, rolls them up, and tucks them away, never throwing any out. "Sometimes when I read back over them I wonder, 'Why did I feel that was important then?' There is a secret way to open the box," she confides, "but I can't tell you!"

The conversation moves to life's purpose. "Sometimes I think about it. I usually don't think about it directly, like asking myself what is the meaning of life. I approach it in smaller, more manageable ways. I think more in terms of values, or choosing different ways of seeing things, or looking at how we contribute to life."

One of Serina's contributions was helping to form a group in her senior year called the Environmental Awareness Team, EAT for short. They produced and sold recycled paper tablets, picked up litter on the island, and planted trees at the school. "I think individuals can make a difference. If you don't think that, life feels pretty hopeless. But the hard part is that change comes slow. It can be kind of annoying. Lots of people don't take the kind of effort we made seriously, but you have to start somewhere. I think we all have some base set of things we believe. You sort of have to. If not, there's nothing there, and it all just kind of blows away.

"I don't believe there is something that controls us, or in the traditional form of God. I believe in evolution, that we've come to be through our own strengths. I do believe in unity, in the force of nature and of us. I think we're just part of nature. It's not like there is a division between nature and people. It's all one.

"I think what we choose to do with our life is what gives it meaning. It's what we make of it. After we die, we become part of the earth again. I think about it in terms of conservation of matter, so we are eternal in some sense. I don't believe we go to the fluffy clouds in the sky. It's a nice thought, but I just can't believe that.

"It's never easy for me to talk about things. I'd like people to know who I am, but it's hard to show them, because it makes me feel vulnerable. I don't feel like people know me very well. That can be isolating. I'm usually not very good at sharing things." Her face brightens. "But it seems like I'm doing okay today!"

Pamela Maresten

The world is ravishing today. Redwing blackbirds are singing down at the big pond. Tulips burst with colors that can't be found in an artist's box. Pamela's land is something to be felt as well as seen. Where does the garden end, where does the bird's song begin? Tall grasses paint the spaces between water and shore. We walk together, past rock outcroppings, ponds, and trees planted long years past. A wooden orchard ladder leans into the arms of an apple tree.

Pamela is like deep, quiet water. Her steps are slow and even. This place *resten*

is sacred to her. "I laid down prayers when we came here. This is where my roots are." When she came, this was all forest, dense and dark. "When we cleared our land for the house, the birds left. It was horrible in that way. I had to forgive myself for what we did, cutting the trees, taking so much away." Her eyes still hold the pain. "I remember the year the birds came back.

"The land is my greatest teacher. I consider my spiritual home where the land and the sea meet. Some days I wake up and wonder, will it be a one-raven or a two-raven morning? I've learned a lot about the source of things and about balance from the land. Air, fire, water…it can so quickly be out of balance. It's like wanting water in the house, but wanting it to come in where *I* want it to, through pipes, not a hole in the roof. Our human ideas can be so strong!"

We walk to the house. Inside the front door, a string of gold Christmas stars loops over a rack of elk antlers. A sleek wooden kayak, handmade by Pamela years ago, hangs suspended from the ceiling beams. Elegant simplicity. A fanciful wooden frog with a carved gold necklace and wonderful wings dangles from a cord, his body making a dance in the air. Outside the window, a wild currant tree seems to slip its blossoms right over the sill into the room.

Much of the wood in this house came off Pamela's land. The beams, the posts, the furniture, the planks on the floor. These planks aren't fancy. Boots have scraped across their chest. They've felt dancing shoes in winter, bare feet in summer. "There is a lot of magic in this house. Amazing gatherings have happened here–music, weddings, prayer meetings, coming-of-age ceremonies–good, powerful gatherings of people."

Over the years Pamela has worked as a gardener, land-scaper, and artist, but the role closest to her heart is the one she calls "artistic director specializing in set design." "I help create and design spaces for special events in people's lives, like weddings or personal ceremonies. You could say I create a bowl, or a boundary space, for what the event is all about, for whatever magic wants to happen. I began this work by doing set design in theater, but it didn't stay there, it moved into community events.

"Right now I'm in a gestation time with work. I'm in-between. It's hard not to have a title, something that says this is who I am, this is me, this is my purpose. God, it's embarrassing! Much of my personal identity used to be through my work in gardening and landscaping. Physical work. I'm making a shift, not doing that anymore. It's difficult to make that change, but it's very important to me. I'm not in our community as much as I used to be when my children were here. There's a certain loss in it. I don't really know how to fit into things right now."

Pamela talks about how that's been, pulling in, spending more time on her own. "It's been a powerful time of intro-spection, but I think I'm ready to meet the world a little more now, to move back into the community, to find a way to combine my beliefs with my experience. I don't know where that is yet. I'm listening. Sometimes I'm anxious about it. The question becomes 'How do we move forward into new territory and create something that we don't know anything about yet?' What I'm learning about is silence, waiting, and patience. Of course I'm uncomfortable with it! It's much easier to be active. That gives some proof you're alive.

"I am aware that two things are strong in me now. First, I try not to get caught up in the fastness of things, not over-load myself. I don't put a lot of things down on the calendar anymore. The doorway to *real life* comes in not being too busy. I realize that time is all there is. It's all we are given. Why would I want to give it away to things that aren't

133

meaningful to me anymore? The other thing I've tried to learn is voluntary simplicity. I want to really live that. It does work, and it's also a lot of work to do. You have to be attentive. I find my mind still wanting things. I have to fight against it, especially when I'm off island, or in the city, or with my family."

Young people seek Pamela out. "I get a lot of juice from that! I love working on the coming-of-age ceremonies, those passages that punctuate our lives. In this community we are committed to each other. We go the long road together. I try to encourage kids' potential, especially kids taking a path that's not mainstream. I've got a lot of experience under my belt. I feel like I can offer some perspective. It's important for kids to learn to honor themselves. We can't take care of our children if we can't take care of ourselves though. How can you ask someone to love you when you can't love yourself?"

Pamela's years show in her words, not her appearance. Her blond hair falls silky past her shoulders. Her feet are bare. Her eyes hold the blue of the sky. Today she wears black slacks and a tunic. It comes as a surprise when she says she turned fifty a few years ago.

Our conversation returns to finding meaning in our lives, addressing the question of why we are here. Pamela smiles broadly, then laughs out loud. "I've thought about it a lot, and you know, *I just don't get it.* It's like a science experiment run amok. I don't get why we're so separate, why we do such harm to each other. I figure it's mystery. When I was young, I used to have loftier ideas. Not anymore. Now I'm not thinking so much about the why; I'm just trying to figure out the *how* of being alive. It's really confusing. That's the part about getting older, you realize there are no absolutes. Nothing is black and white. It's all just *fuzz.*" Here comes that laugh again–big, honest, full. "I've even started painting that way. Sometimes I don't make clean lines at all, I just let it blur."

Pamela drops into a quiet place. It's clear she's giving this question more time inside. "I do have a high sense of personal honor about living on the planet right now. It is about how we walk and act, what we think about. If we could really discover how to tap into clearness and operate from there, it would be a big turnaround." She pauses. "But why would we need to be here, to be alive, if we already knew how to do that?"

I laid down prayers when we came here.
This is where my roots are.

"I want to tell you lots about my life! I've made up so many stories, and made it so gaudy! My stories always have at least a *little* kernel of truth in them, but you have to embroider. A shirt can be very ordinary and dull, but once it's embroidered it becomes beautiful and rich."

Hildegarde whips off her glasses mid-thought and, leaning over the sink, runs tap water over the lenses. She mops them off with a paper towel. "You must meet Brujo! El Amor Brujo, actually. That means Love Magician in Spanish." Hearing his name, a 140-pound, jet-black, pink-tongued, panting Rottweiler pops up from behind the half-wall between the kitchen and dining room and drops two plate-sized paws over the divider. I take a fast step back. "Oh, Brujo is perfectly harmless," Hildegarde laughs. "He's my husband Bill's pride and joy!" She pops a Milk Bone in the dog's huge mouth. "And here is my Miss Rhoda. Hello, beloved!" Her prim little Welsh corgi wags up for a treat.

Hildegarde is a treat herself, like one of those party favor balls from childhood birthdays: pull the paper ribbon, and trinkets and surprises spill out. Today she wears a long, beaded necklace, knit hat with silk roses tucked into the band, her trademark purple scarf, sweats, and jogging shoes.

When are you happiest?

"I think people make me happiest. I truly love people. I must tell you, in that way I'm lucky. But I don't like humanity. No. Humanity is a mess. I don't love them. I love individual people. I know some who love humanity, but hate people."

Did you and Bill think of having children?

"No, thank God! If we'd raised children, they would have been delinquents; we would have been visiting them in jail. Just look at our dogs! Also, it was the Depression. You didn't think of having children so much then."

One of your roles in this community is a sounding board for young people. Many come to you for grounding.

"Isn't that nuts?!" Her eyes are smiling. "I think they come because I love them. When kids are eighteen, they need their parents more than ever. It's a hell of a time in life. The boys still look unfinished, a little wormy. I think kids at this age get forgotten a lot. Often they're so miserable. It's wonderful and terrible to be that age. They want to hold onto their family ties, and yet they're trying to untie those connections at the same time. At eighteen, kids need the assurance they still belong."

What about guiding principles?

"One is hug people. Another must be laughter. I learned very young to make people laugh. Comedy was part of the game. My mother said you better have a good laugh every day. She also taught me you can be sick for three days, but then go out and help someone."

As a young woman Hildegarde attended art school in California. Her large canvases hang on the walls—paintings of birds, dogs, flowers, friends. She writes short stories too. "I make verbs out of nouns." She's talking about her writing, but it's a good description of the way she lives. "Slip-slide. Don't you just love double words? Fiddle-faddle. She slip-

137

slided past and fiddle-faddled about! Isn't that a lovely notion?"

Will you tell your age?

"Good God, yes! I'm proud of it. I'm eighty-one! Here's what I think about aging. You struggle until you're seventy; then the job really starts. Then you have to struggle with yourself. You begin to realize you can't blame anybody else. That's when you begin to be a little more tolerant. It's a little like gardening. You weed and weed all day, then turn around and find even more weeds behind you.

"You get really lonely when you get old. Yes, I am lonely. I'm so delighted when I get a phone call. I'm a phone freak. It's a wonderful instrument. At my age, a person's chances are all past. You're lonesome. You have your past to think about, but you don't have that level of activity any more. But it's not all bad. I have my dogs! They may get bored with me, but at least they don't talk back. I watch television, like any old idiot. I think I'm a damn fool. But I must tell you I think old fools are good too. They're a need in this world.

"Some people think I'm eccentric. I'm really very normal...sort of! People who tend to be straightforward like me can be scary. They think because I'm old, I must be saying things that are true. There are a hell of a lot of things I'm telling you even now that are sheer nonsense!" For a moment a serious, steady look lights her eyes. "It's because life *is* nonsensical. It hurts too much if it's not. It's as simple as that. Now that's probably the most honest thing I've said today.

"What I'm saying is you better have plenty of laughter in your life and you better take things light. Have fun with life. Enjoy! Enjoy! Enjoy! I tell my friends, 'Enjoy your misery too; it may not last.'"

How should I capture you on the page, Hildegarde?

"You could describe me as a fat, pudgy old lady who you don't expect to say 'Oh shit!'" She leans forward. "I can say that word because in Swedish it isn't a swear word. It means dirt. That's why I've always felt perfectly comfortable using it. Or you could say I'm sophisticated. Sometimes I think I'm sophisticated, but I may not be at all. People with round eyes don't look sophisticated. Insightful might be right. And I do have self-honesty, though I don't show it all the time. I can be a fraud, but not when someone's hurting. Then I never am. My friends are too important to me."

Do you want people to know anything else about you?

"No. People will never know me anyhow unless they know themselves first. That's the way it works, isn't it?" A smile breaks over her face like sweet surprise. "I think maybe because I like other people, I can like myself."

What do you think happens after we die?

"I don't know what's in the afterlife. I know an awful lot of people who are dead in *this* life. Haven't you run into them? Here's what I think about death: people are in another place, you just can't see them. When you're sad, you can turn to their spirit and really talk with them. I talk to my mother more now than when she first died in 1952."

What will you think on your deathbed?

"I'll say, 'Oh shit! Is that all there is? Gosh, it was a short session. It didn't last long enough!' I already have my plot at the cemetery. It's right near the pathway, so I'll get noticed! I want my memorial service to be held toward evening so there can be fireworks. I hope they'll have at least two Roman candles! I wonder, will they allow it? I've always thought that would be *such* fun.

"On my headstone I just want my name, Hildegarde. No other words. And I want a bronze feather. In other words: she was here...and she dropped a feather."

Garden Party

When Gail turned forty-five, she gave herself a birthday party. I think that takes courage. I'm the type that starts dropping hints about a month out, then secretly hope my pals will "remember" when my day rolls around. I like her approach better.

She asked her friends to give her the gift of their time. With all that had been going on in her life since she became single again, her large, beautiful vegetable garden had gone to weeds. Gail invited about forty of us to come help get it ready for planting. "Afternoon Garden Party. Help me celebrate my birthday. Bring your gloves, hoes, shovels, and children!" the Xeroxed invitation read, promising her famous cooking after the work was done.

The garden really was a tangle. Lark and Corrie unloaded their rototiller from the truck. Heather carried up a bucket of herb starts for planting. As adults grabbed shovels and rakes out of their trunks, children poured into the yard, spontaneously adding their own tangle of wrestling arms and legs to the commotion.

Like a bumblebee going flower to flower, the Birthday Girl buzzed around, getting us organized, supervising the action, asking a few adults to help the children move rocks, pointing out for us non-garden types the difference between a weed and a flower.

As I turned the soil with my shovel, I kept thinking of Amish barn-raisings…everyone doing his or her own piece, and after a while the barn stands proud in the field. Gail's party worked exactly like that. By 4 o'clock, the weeds, thistles, and blackberry brambles were cleared away. The black earth of the raised beds, now turned and weeded, lay in rich mounds ready for planting. The kids showed their new rockery wall. The garden gate was back on its hinges. The deer fencing was mended.

Other things mended too. Two women over by the far gate rejoined the party, arms looped around each other's waist.

Gail's grilled fresh salmon was delicious that late after-noon. The tables overflowed with her salads, side dishes, and desserts. I filled my paper plate, poured a glass of Chardonnay, and found a place to sit quietly with a friend.

Evening was turning the pond pink. Last light was finding its way through the branches of the cherry trees in the little orchard. I wanted to savor the day. The whole event had been new for me. Fresh. Important.

Gail's party sticks with me now, two years later. I admire her self-confidence in throwing this little bash, and I love the model it gave me: in a society that overvalues independence, it takes courage to give interdependence a chance, to be willing to ask for help.

I learned something that day that my grandparents probably knew in their life on the Alberta prairie…relying on each other is sweet medicine. It binds us, deepens us, connects us. It honors the trust friends hold one for another. Working and playing together at Gail's party that spring day, we, of course, were the ones who received the gift.

Transitions

During the four years of writing this book, many changes came to our island and the people who live here. Mark Brown lost his wife, Lois. In addition to Sally Bill, whose memorial is detailed here, we also said goodbye to Mary La Porte and Dort Horne.

While these wonderful women often feel as close as the morning breeze, they are also profoundly missed. Their legacies of love, wisdom, and vitality remain woven deeply into our lives. Godspeed.

And Julie Miller's baby arrived! She and her husband Dennis named their healthy, beautiful son Truman. Here he is now…

Acknowledgments

We've both felt, all along, that we were more midwives to this book than authors of it. We interviewed thirty-two people, but countless others helped shape the vision of the book, gave moral support, read drafts, and shared their talents and expertise along the way. The kindness of these friends and neighbors has taught us firsthand about the power and blessing of community.

Special thanks to Dorothy Conway, Nancy Atkins, Pat Sterne, Linda Hemans, Shannon K. Jacobs, and Phyllis Potter for donating their considerable editing talents to polish this work. Bravo! Jeremy Snapp and M. Cathy Angel gave us invaluable help with the publishing process and Beth Black worked magic with her remarkable marketing ideas. On the photographic front, thanks to Liz and Jeff Malinoff for the use of their home darkroom and to Steve Horn for his professional help. Maripat Murphy did a great job on the final edit. Artists Bob Lanphear and Piia Pretz of Lanphear Design presented these words and photographs with rare beauty and life on the page. Finally, our love to Alie Smaalders, mentor, editor, and heartfriend who encouraged us every step of the way.

144